ACT LIKE JESUS

How Can I Put
My Faith Into Action?

STUDY GUIDE | EIGHT SESSIONS

RANDY FRAZEE

ZONDERVAN

Act Like Jesus Study Guide
Copyright © 2020 by Randy Frazee

This title is also available as a Zondervan ebook.

Requests for information should be addressed to: Zondervan, 3900 Sparks Dr. SE, Grand Rapids, Michigan 49546

Portions of this guide were adapted from the *Believe Study Guide* (9780310826118) and from *Think, Act, Be Like Jesus* (9780310250173) by Randy Frazee.

ISBN 978-0-310-11903-6 (softcover)
ISBN 978-0-310-11904-3 (ebook)

First printing April 2020 / Printed in the United States of America

CONTENTS

HOW TO USE THIS GUIDE

Scope and Sequence

The goal of every follower of Jesus Christ is to become more like him, but how do you know where to start? What does it really mean to be a disciple of Jesus? The objective of *Act Like Jesus*—the second in a series of three small-group studies—is to start the process toward transforming your behaviors so your actions will more closely match the actions of Christ. This study guide (and the related video) will help you assess your spiritual life, pinpoint areas that need special attention, and give you tools to help you grow. The previous study in this series, *Think Like Jesus*, focused on the core beliefs of the Christian faith. This study will focus on the foundational practices of the Christian life. The final study, *Be Like Jesus*, will focus on Christlike virtues. May God bless you as you seek him through this experience!

Session Outline

Each session is divided into two parts. In the group section, you and your group will begin by watching a short video teaching from Randy Frazee and follow along with the note-taking outline that has been provided. You will then recite the key verse, the key idea, and engage in some guided group discussion through the questions provided. At the end of the group time, you will be given real-life scenarios of people who struggle with their faith. Using the key applications from your study guide, your group will be challenged to think of ways to encourage the people within these case studies. Finally, you will close the group with a time of prayer.

Personal Study

At the end of the group section, you will find a series of readings and study questions for you to go through on your own during the week. Each of these sections will challenge you to consider a key question about the topic, think through a key idea, and then consider a key application regarding the difference it should make in your life. You will also be given four statements to help you evaluate the alignment of your life with the key idea and asked to take action by memorizing each session's key idea and key verse. **The personal study is a critical component in helping you see how the beliefs you are studying are reflected in the pages of the Bible, so be sure to complete this study during the week before your next group meeting.**

Group Size

Act Like Jesus is designed to be experienced in a group setting such as a Bible study, Sunday school class, or any small-group gathering. To ensure everyone has enough time to participate in discussions, it is recommended that large groups watch the video together and then break up into smaller groups of four to six people for discussion.

Materials Needed

Each participant should have his or her own study guide. Although the course can be fully experienced with just the video and study guide, participants are also encouraged to have a copy of *Believe: Living the Story of the Bible to Become Like Jesus*, which includes selections from the *New International Version* that relate to each week's session. Reading *Believe* as you go through the study will provide even deeper insights and make the journey even richer and more meaningful.

Facilitation

Each group should appoint a leader who is responsible for starting the video and for keeping track of time during discussions and activities. Leaders may also read questions aloud and monitor discussions, prompting participants to respond and ensuring that everyone has the opportunity to participate. (For more thorough instructions, see the Leader's Guide included at the back of this guide.)

Session 1

HOW DO I WORSHIP GOD?

A simple definition for the practice of worship is "attributing worth to someone or something." Worship is not an earthly event you attend but rather a heavenly activity in which you take part. As a Christian, in your personal and corporate worship of God, you are attributing or ascribing worth to him . . . and to him alone. Regardless of the method of praise—whether singing, speaking, or other expression—you are both believing of him and communicating to him, "God, you are worthy." You are declaring he is worthy—and everything and anything else is not. Worship is the catalyst that moves you from believing in God with your head to a belief that sits deep in your heart. It changes who you are and your knowledge of who God is.

VIDEO TEACHING NOTES

Welcome to session one of *Act Like Jesus*. If this is your first time together as a group, take a moment to introduce yourselves to each other. As you watch the video, use the following outline to record some of the main points. (The answer key is found at the end of the session.)

- **Key Question**: How do I honor God in the way he _____?

- **Key Idea**: I worship God for _____ he is and what he has _____ for me.

- **Key Verse**: "Come, let us sing for joy to the LORD; let us shout aloud to the Rock of our salvation. Let us come before him with _____ and extol him with music and song" (Psalm 95:1-2).

- **(Key Application #1)**: I _____ _____ acknowledge God for who he is and what he has done for me.

- **(Key Application #2)**: I worship God, _____ _____ and _____, with the songs I sing, the words I speak, and the way I live my life.

- **(Key Application #3)**: When I attribute _____ _____ to God as a child of God, unmerited worth is attributed to me.

GETTING STARTED

Begin your discussion by reciting the key verse and key idea together as a group. On your first attempt, use your notes if you need help. On your second attempt, try to state them completely from memory.

KEY VERSE: "Come, let us sing for joy to the LORD; let us shout aloud to the Rock of our salvation. Let us come before him with thanksgiving and extol him with music and song" (Psalm 95:1–2).

KEY IDEA: I worship God for who he is and what he has done for me.

GROUP DISCUSSION

As a group, discuss your thoughts and feelings about the following declarations. Which statements are easy to declare with certainty? Which are more challenging? Why?

- I thank God daily for who he is and what he is doing in my life.
- I attend religious services and worship with other believers each week.

- I give God the credit for all that I am and all that I possess.
- I am not ashamed for others to know that I worship God.

Based on your group's dynamics and spiritual maturity, choose the two to three questions that will lead to the best discussion about this week's key idea.

1. What are some ways you can list of how worship can be expressed to God?

2. What about God's character compels you to give him your worship?

3. Which worship song lyrics best describe your thoughts and feelings about God?

4. In what ways do you see your fellow group members expressing worship to God?

_____

_____

_____

_____

Read Matthew 23:1–28 and choose one to two questions that will lead to the greatest discussion in your group.

1. In what ways can worship become a heartless ritual?

_____

_____

_____

2. What do you learn from Jesus' rebuke of the Pharisees? How can you keep from making the same mistake?

_____

_____

_____

_____

3. What has God done in your life that has produced a desire to worship him?

_____

_____

_____

CASE STUDY

Use the following case study as a model for a real-life situation where you might put this week's key idea into practice.

> You became friends with Tiago three years ago when your sons started playing soccer together. As you cheer on the boys, your conversations often lead to serious topics, such as faith, politics, and college football. Tiago describes himself as a spiritual person who keeps his beliefs private. He occasionally says, "I've never felt the need to make my faith public. What's the point?"

Using the following key applications from this session, what could you say or do to help Tiago?

KEY APPLICATION #1: I daily acknowledge God for who he is and what he has done for me.

KEY APPLICATION #2: I worship God, privately and corporately, with the songs I sing, the words I speak, and the way I live my life.

KEY APPLICATION #3: When I attribute worth to God as a child of God, unmerited worth is attributed to me.

CLOSING PRAYER

Close your time together with prayer. Share your prayer requests with one another. Ask God to help you put this week's key idea into practice.

FOR NEXT WEEK

Before your next group meeting, be sure to read through the following personal study and complete the exercises.

VIDEO NOTES ANSWER KEY

deserves / who, done / thanksgiving / daily / privately, corporately / worth

PERSONAL STUDY

Every session in this guide contains a personal study to help you make meaningful connections between your life and what you are learning each week. Take some time after your group meeting each week to read through this section and complete the personal study. In total, the personal study should take about one hour to complete. Some people like to spread it out, devoting about ten to fifteen minutes a day. Others choose one larger block of time during the week to work through the entire personal study in one sitting. There is no right or wrong way to do this! Just choose a plan that best fits your needs and schedule from week to week, and then allow the Scripture to take root in your heart.

KEY QUESTION
HOW DO I HONOR GOD IN THE WAY HE DESERVES?

True worship honors God in the way he deserves. It declares our belief that God is the one true God. It expresses our belief in God's care and acknowledges he has provided the way for us to be made right with him. Our worship is based on the fact that the Bible directs our beliefs and actions and that our worth and significance come from God. As we recognize him as the head of the church and believe he loves all people, we respond to others with compassion—because that is who God is. We honor him as the one who is the owner of all things, including us.

Worshiping God can be expressed in many different forms and diverse environments, but it is what we believe in our hearts that matters to God. Throughout the Bible, God's people demonstrated their devotion to him with singing, dancing, sacrifices, and public and private prayer. But what is most important to God is the motivation that directs our actions.

God wants us to put him before all else and honor him above everything else—including ourselves. Or course, putting God first can be challenging, because there is a cost involved. However, we must acknowledge that God *deserves* our worship, and we must choose to honor him at all times in every situation. Our motivation for worship is based on who God is and what he has done for us. This is the heart of worship that honors God in the way he deserves.

> *Come, let us sing for joy to the LORD;*
> *let us shout aloud to the Rock of our salvation.*
> *Let us come before him with thanksgiving*
> *and extol him with music and song* (Psalm 95:1–2).

> *Therefore, brothers and sisters, since we have confidence to enter the Most Holy Place by the blood of Jesus, by a new and living way opened for us through the curtain, that is, his body, and since we have a great priest over the house of God, let us draw near to God with a sincere heart and with the full assurance that faith brings, having our hearts sprinkled to cleanse us from a guilty conscience and having our bodies washed with pure water. Let us hold unswervingly to the hope we profess, for he who promised is faithful* (Hebrews 10:19–23).

1. What attitude should you have when you worship God?

_____

_____

_____

_____

2. Why does God deserve your worship?

_____

_____

_____

_____

KEY IDEA

I WORSHIP GOD FOR WHO HE IS AND WHAT HE HAS DONE FOR ME

Jesus said, "True worshipers will worship the Father in the Spirit and in truth, for they are the kind of worshipers the Father seeks. God is spirit, and his worshipers must worship in the Spirit and in truth" (John 4:23–24). True worship is not about being at a precise location but about having an intimate spiritual longing. God seeks worshipers who, through the power of his Spirit, will attribute worth to him in any location and for the right reasons—because he is truth.

In the psalms, we read that we are to "ascribe to the LORD the glory due his name" and "worship the LORD in the splendor of his holiness" (Psalm 29:2). We are to "extol the LORD" and "praise him" (Psalm 109:30). Our motivation for this centers around what God had done for us and our response to his grace. God, not our circumstances, drives true worship. We are not called to merely go through the motions but to *authentically* worship God from our hearts.

Worshiping the one true God for who he is and what he has done is something we can share with the world. We can worship God from our hearts through every single breath, expression, thought, and activity of our lives. Doing this habitually—and also in community—will surely lead us closer to the great and gracious God of the universe.

> Let the peace of Christ rule in your hearts, since as members of one body you were called to peace. And be thankful. Let the message of Christ dwell among you richly as you teach and admonish one another with all wisdom through psalms, hymns, and songs from the Spirit, singing to God with gratitude in your hearts. And whatever you do, whether in word or deed, do it all in the name of the Lord Jesus, giving thanks to God the Father through him (Colossians 3:15–17).

> Shout for joy to the LORD, all the earth.
>> Worship the LORD with gladness;
>> come before him with joyful songs.
> Know that the LORD is God.
>> It is he who made us, and we are his;
>> we are his people, the sheep of his pasture
> (Psalm 100:1–3).

> Rejoice always, pray continually, give thanks in all circumstances; for this is God's will for you in Christ Jesus (1 Thessalonians 5:16–18).

1. What attitudes and actions constitute proper worship?

   _____

   _____

   _____

   _____

2. What are the benefits of worshiping with other believers?

   _____

   _____

   _____

   _____

KEY APPLICATION
WHAT DIFFERENCE THIS MAKES

Since the fall of humankind in the garden of Eden, our greatest struggle has been the desire to be our own god. While most of us would not wish to have the responsibility and burden of calling the shots for the entire world, we *do* want to be the god of our own lives. We want to do what we want, when we want, where we want, and with whom we want.

When we engage in worship, we crawl off the *throne* of God (where we do not belong) and crawl onto the *altar* of God (where we do belong). In this exchange, we surrender control and attribute worth to God—and he, in turn, attributes his worth back to us as his children. Worship expresses the relationship we have with God. The stronger the relationship and the deeper the intimacy, the greater the worship. This leads to us having a deeper love for God.

Worship is connected to our hearts as believers. Our deep respect, awe, joy, gratitude, and relief at God's blessings may overwhelm us to the point where we don't care about anyone or anything except worshiping God in the Spirit and in truth. The point is not about how we worship but about our hearts! It is about how much love and devotion exist in our lives for God. Someone in quiet meditation can be just as deep in adoration of God as the one whose voice is raised—and vice versa. True worship is simply a reflection of our hearts as believers.

> *Wearing a linen ephod, David was dancing before the LORD with all his might, while he and all Israel were bringing up the ark of the LORD with shouts and the sound of trumpets.*
>
> *As the ark of the LORD was entering the City of David, Michal daughter of Saul watched from a window. And when she saw King David leaping and dancing before the LORD, she despised him in her heart. . . . When David returned home to bless his household, Michal daughter of Saul came out to meet him and said, "How the king of Israel has distinguished himself today, going around half-naked in full view of the slave girls of his servants as any vulgar fellow would!"*
>
> *David said to Michal, "It was before the LORD, who chose me rather than your father or anyone from his house when he appointed me ruler over the LORD's people Israel—I will celebrate before the LORD* (2 Samuel 6:14–16, 20–21).

> *May these words of my mouth and this meditation of my heart*
>   *be pleasing in your sight,*
> *LORD, my Rock and my Redeemer* (Psalm 19:14).

1. How do you see the hearts of other believers displayed through worship?

_____

_____

_____

_____

_____

2. What happens when your focus is on the *means* of expressing worship rather than the *content* of your worship?

_____

_____

_____

_____

EVALUATE

As you conclude this personal study, use a scale of 1–6 to rate how strongly you believe the following statements (1 = no belief at all, 6 = complete confidence):

_____ I thank God daily for who he is and what he is doing in my life.

_____ I attend religious services and worship with other believers each week.

_____ I give God the credit for all that I am and all that I possess.

_____ I am not ashamed for others to know that I worship God.

TAKE ACTION

Memorizing Scripture is a valuable discipline for all believers to exercise. Spend a few minutes each day committing this week's key verse to memory.

KEY VERSE: "Come, let us sing for joy to the LORD; let us shout aloud to the Rock of our salvation. Let us come before him with thanksgiving and extol him with music and song" (Psalm 95:1–2).

Recite this week's key idea out loud. As you do, ask yourself, *Does my life reflect this statement?*

KEY IDEA: I worship God for who he is and what he has done for me.

Answer the following questions to help you apply this week's key idea to your own life.

1. How could this practice express itself in your life?

2. What visible attributes can be found in someone committed to the practice of worship?

_____

_____

_____

_____

_____

_____

3. What impedes your ability to make worship part of your everyday activity? How can you overcome this obstacle?

_____

_____

_____

_____

_____

_____

4. What step can you take this week to give God more honor and praise?

_____

_____

_____

_____

_____

_____

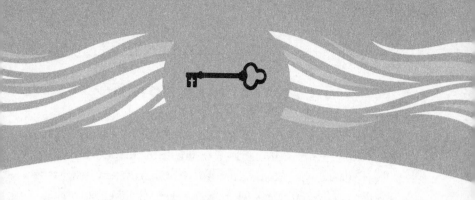

Session 2

WHY DO I NEED TO PRAY?

When you engage in the discipline of prayer, you convey—as well as reinforce—your belief in *God*. When you cast your cares on him, lay your burdens before him, and share your hearts with him, you reinforce and express the truth that he is a *personal God*. You pray, believing and trusting that he is involved in and cares about your daily life. When you ask God to give you direction, you are reinforcing and expressing the belief of *stewardship*. Because God is the owner of everything, you go to him for the next step in every walk of life. The practices of Jesus connect to the beliefs of Jesus. In this practice, Christ calls you to pray as he prayed.

VIDEO TEACHING NOTES

Welcome to session two of *Act Like Jesus*. If there are any new members in your group, take a moment to introduce yourselves to each other. Spend a few minutes sharing any insights or questions about last week's personal study. Then start the video and use the following outline to record some of the main points. (The answer key is found at the end of the session.)

- **Key Question**: How do I grow by _____ _____ with God?

- **Key Idea**: I pray to God to _____ him, to _____ direction for my life, and to _____ my requests before him.

- "Watch _____ and then simply do what he does."

- It is completely _____ for us to lay our requests before God.

- Like Jesus, we should seek to _____ our lives to God's will, versus asking God to align his life to our will.

- **Key Verse**: "If I had cherished sin in my heart, the LORD would not have listened; but God has surely listened and has heard my _____. Praise be to God, who has not rejected my prayer or withheld his love from me!" (Psalm 66:18–20).

- **(Key Application #1):** I _____ to align my life to God's will.

- **(Key Application #2):** I pray to lay my _____ before God to find peace.

- **(Key Application #3):** I won't make any major decisions in my life without _____ God through prayer.

GETTING STARTED

Begin your discussion by reciting the key verse and key idea together as a group. On your first attempt, use your notes if you need help. On your second attempt, try to state them completely from memory.

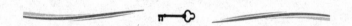

KEY VERSE: "If I had cherished sin in my heart, the LORD would not have listened; but God has surely listened and has heard my prayer. Praise be to God, who has not rejected my prayer or withheld his love from me!" (Psalm 66:18–20).

KEY IDEA: I pray to God to know him, to find direction for my life, and to lay my requests before him.

GROUP DISCUSSION

As a group, discuss your thoughts and feelings about the following declarations. Which statements are easy to declare with certainty? Which are more challenging? Why?

- I seek God's will through prayer.
- I regularly confess my sins to God.
- Prayer is a central part of my daily life.
- I seek to grow closer to God by listening to him in prayer.

Based on your group's dynamics and spiritual maturity, choose the two to three questions that will lead to the best discussion about this week's key idea.

1. What aspect of prayer do you find to be the most challenging? Helpful? Rewarding?

2. How has the act of prayer helped you know and understand God better?

3. In what ways have you seen and experienced the power of prayer at work?

4. What are some different ways you have seen God answer specific prayer requests?

Read Matthew 26:36–39, Mark 1:32–35, and Luke 6:12–16, and then choose one or two questions that will lead to the greatest discussion in your group.

1. What inspires you when you examine Jesus' dependence on, confidence in, and commitment to unceasing prayer?

2. How has prayer helped you navigate the tough decisions that life has thrown your way?

3. What is one aspect of Jesus' prayer life that you would like to emulate?

CASE STUDY

Use the following case study as a model for a real-life situation where you might put this week's key idea into practice.

> Gabe has been offered an opportunity to join an exciting start-up company. His existing job pays well and provides great benefits, but he has been bored and uninspired by the mundane tasks he performs. This new opportunity could bring the excitement and creativity he has been longing to find, but it comes with significant financial risk.

Using the following key applications from this session, what could you say or do to help Gabe?

KEY APPLICATION #1: I pray to align my life to God's will.

KEY APPLICATION #2: I pray to lay my burdens before God to find peace.

KEY APPLICATION #3: I won't make any major decisions in my life without seeking God through prayer.

CLOSING PRAYER

Close your time together with prayer. Share your prayer requests with one another. Ask God to help you put this week's key idea into practice.

FOR NEXT WEEK

Before your next group meeting, be sure to read through the following personal study and complete the exercises.

VIDEO NOTES ANSWER KEY

communicating / know, find, lay / Jesus / acceptable / align /
prayer / pray / burdens / seeking

PERSONAL STUDY

Last week, you examined the practice of worship. Perhaps your definition of worship was expanded and enhanced through what you learned. Before your next group meeting, complete the following study. Allow the Scripture to challenge you about what it means to communicate with God.

KEY QUESTION
HOW DO I GROW BY COMMUNICATING WITH GOD?

To learn how to act like Jesus in the area of prayer, we must understand Jesus' priority of prayer. He went away from everyone to be alone. No distractions, no other voices . . . no one but the Father and him. Then he prayed—sharing his heart with God and listening to him.

We don't know how long Jesus prayed or what he talked to God about. But we do know that he dedicated time for communication with the Father before he went about his day. As we read in Luke 6:12–13, "Jesus went out to a mountainside to pray, and spent the night praying to God. When morning came, he called his disciples to him and chose twelve of them." Spending time in prayer gave Jesus the strength and guidance he needed to fulfill his purpose on earth.

We tend to have a narrow view of what it means to spend time communicating with God. It is important not to view focused moments of prayer as our "God time" and then make the rest of our day all about *us*. Rather, our focused time with God sets the tone for our day, starting an ongoing dialogue with our heavenly Father that will continue through the ups and downs of daily life. If Jesus needed to spend time alone with the Father, talking to him and listening to him, how much more should we prioritize this practice!

> *Very early in the morning, while it was still dark, Jesus got up, left the house and went off to a solitary place, where he prayed* (Mark 1:35).

> *Jesus went out to a mountainside to pray, and spent the night praying to God. When morning came, he called his disciples to him and chose twelve of them* (Luke 6:12–13).

> *Rejoice always, pray continually, give thanks in all circumstances; for this is God's will for you in Christ Jesus* (1 Thessalonians 5:16–18).

1. What can you learn from this pattern of prayer that Jesus demonstrated?

   _____

   _____

   _____

   _____

2. What are your current patterns of prayer?

   _____

   _____

   _____

   _____

KEY IDEA

I PRAY TO KNOW HIM, FIND DIRECTION FOR MY LIFE, AND LAY MY REQUESTS BEFORE HIM

We find one of Jesus' prayers in John 17. A remarkable aspect of this dialogue is that Jesus prays for *everyone* who will ever believe in him. This example of Jesus' prayer can instruct us in how to pray and encourage us by revealing what Jesus asks the Father on our behalf.

Jesus also gives us examples of how *not* to pray. In Matthew 6:5, he states that we are not to pray "like the hypocrites," who only practiced prayer as an outward display of religiousness, and for human approval. Rather, Jesus taught his followers to pray that God's kingdom would come and his will would be done (see verse 10). Jesus' model prayer for his followers was concise yet detailed (see verses 9–13). Religious and flowery words were not necessary or required—just honest and open requests.

In the Gospels, we eavesdrop by the door of heaven and hear Jesus taking his greatest burden to God: the reality of the cross. We see God answer not in the way Jesus might have wanted but in a way that provided for him (see Luke 22:41–43). We can thus be encouraged that though God will not always deliver us *from* our circumstances, he will deliver us *through* our circumstances by giving us what we need in order to accomplish what he asks us to do.

It is through prayer that we take God up on his "open door" policy and speak with him directly. What an amazing privilege! As we do this, we can be assured that he is not threatened by our questions or doubts. We don't have to put on a false persona to please him, because he allows us to be honest about our fears, our feelings of isolation, and our disappointments. When we express our hearts to him, we witness his personal involvement in our lives.

> *If I had cherished sin in my heart,*
> *the LORD would not have listened;*
> *but God has surely listened*
> *and has heard my prayer.*
> *Praise be to God,*
> *who has not rejected my prayer*
> *or withheld his love from me!* (Psalm 66:18–20).

> *"My prayer is not for them alone. I pray also for those who will believe in me through their message, that all of them may be one, Father, just as you are in me and I am in you. May they also be in us so that the world may believe that you have sent me"* (John 17:20–21).

> *Going a little farther, he fell with his face to the ground and prayed, "My Father, if it is possible, may this cup be taken from me. Yet not as I will, but as you will"* (Matthew 26:39).

1. What does spending time in prayer teach you about God's character?

   _____

   _____

   _____

   _____

   _____

   _____

2. What principles of prayer does Jesus provide to you in the Bible?

_____

_____

_____

_____

_____

KEY APPLICATION
WHAT DIFFERENCE THIS MAKES

The psalmists consistently addressed the topic of prayer. They coupled humility with boldness and awe with confidence—not in themselves, but in God. The psalmists inspired and challenged us to go before God and speak to him about the deep need in our lives. This confidence is based on a knowledge of God and his concern for his children.

While the word *prayer* creates a great deal of religious connotation for some and intimidation for others, we must remember an amazing truth: we are being invited to speak with and listen to our Creator and Redeemer. He is not distant . . . and he is listening to us. He does not keep us from going to him but invites us to come to him.

Prayer is a key spiritual practice to help us process difficult events in our lives—to move the reality of our identity in Christ from our heads to our hearts. As we pray psalms of lament, speaking honestly to God, we hear him whisper his loving invitation to walk through life with us and show us his direction for us. As we sit in extended moments of silence, when we don't know what else to say or how to pray, God begins speaking back to us—directly to our spirits—encouraging us and showing us his purposes.

Prayer is a conversation with God. We lay our honest requests before God yet clarify, as Jesus did, that we want God's will to be done over our will. We trust his way to be good and right. As we rest in the presence of God, he speaks and shows us his will in his perfect timing.

I call on you, my God, for you will answer me; turn your ear to me and hear my prayer (Psalm 17:6).

The Lord is near. Do not be anxious about anything, but in every situation, by prayer and petition, with thanksgiving, present your requests to God. And the peace of God, which transcends all understanding, will guard your hearts and your minds in Christ Jesus (Philippians 4:5–7).

Jesus told this parable: "Two men went up to the temple to pray, one a Pharisee and the other a tax collector. The Pharisee stood by himself and prayed: 'God, I thank you that I am not like other people—robbers, evildoers, adulterers—or even like this tax collector. I fast twice a week and give a tenth of all I get.'

"But the tax collector stood at a distance. He would not even look up to heaven, but beat his breast and said, 'God, have mercy on me, a sinner.'

"I tell you that this man, rather than the other, went home justified before God. For all those who exalt themselves will be humbled, and those who humble themselves will be exalted" (Luke 18:9–14).

1. In what ways does spending time in prayer help you to know God?

   _____

   _____

   _____

2. How does prayer help you find direction in life and make decisions?

   _____

   _____

EVALUATE

As you conclude this personal study, use a scale of 1–6 to rate how strongly you believe the following statements (1 = no belief at all, 6 = complete confidence):

_____ I seek God's will through prayer.

_____ I regularly confess my sins to God.

_____ Prayer is a central part of my daily life.

_____ I seek to grow closer to God by listening to him in prayer.

TAKE ACTION

Memorizing Scripture is a valuable discipline for all believers to exercise. Spend a few minutes each day committing this week's key verse to memory.

KEY VERSE: "If I had cherished sin in my heart, the LORD would not have listened; but God has surely listened and has heard my prayer. Praise be to God, who has not rejected my prayer or withheld his love from me!" (Psalm 66:18–20).

Recite this week's key idea out loud. As you do, ask yourself, *Does my life reflect this statement?*

KEY IDEA: I pray to God to know him, to find direction for my life, and to lay my requests before him.

Answer the following questions to help you apply this week's key idea to your own life.

1. How could this practice be applied in your life?

2. What visible attributes can be found in someone who regularly connects with God through prayer?

3. What impedes your ability to communicate with God?
   How can you overcome those obstacles?

   _____

   _____

   _____

   _____

   _____

   _____

   _____

4. What step can you take this week to develop your connection with God through prayer?

   _____

   _____

   _____

   _____

   _____

   _____

   _____

Session 3

HOW DO I STUDY THE BIBLE?

The author of Hebrews writes, "The word of God is...sharper than any double-edged sword, it penetrates even to dividing soul and spirit, joints and marrow; it judges the thoughts and attitudes of the heart" (4:12). Scripture is more powerful than any sword, but it works in much the same way. As you hold God's Word before you, it can cut through any and every issue, dividing each into good and evil, righteous and wrong, showing you what you are to do and how to live. Like a sword, God's Word can be used as an offensive weapon in helping you to grow and mature as well as a defensive device to protect you against oncoming evil.

VIDEO TEACHING NOTES

Welcome to session three of *Act Like Jesus*. Spend a few minutes sharing any insights or questions about last week's personal study. Then start the video and use the following outline to record some of the main points. (The answer key is found at the end of the session.)

- **Key Question:** _____ do I study God's Word?

- **Key Idea:** I study the Bible to _____ God and his _____ and to find _____ for my daily life.

- "Whoever has ears to hear, let them _____ _____" (Mark 4:9).

- **Key Verse:** "For the word of God is alive and active. Sharper than any double-edged sword, it penetrates even to dividing soul and spirit, joints and marrow; it judges the thoughts and _____ _____ of the heart." (Hebrews 4:12)

- The Bible can go deep if the _____ _____ is willing to receive it.

- **(Key Application #1):** Keep your heart soft and _____ to God's Word.

- **(Key Application #2):** Understand the one _____ _____ of the Bible.

- (Key Application #3): Study God's Word in _____

  _____.

- (Key Application #4): _____
  God's Word.

GETTING STARTED

Begin your discussion by reciting the key verse and key idea together as a group. On your first attempt, use your notes if you need help. On your second attempt, try to state them completely from memory.

KEY VERSE: "For the word of God is alive and active. Sharper than any double-edged sword, it penetrates even to dividing soul and spirit, joints and marrow; it judges the thoughts and attitudes of the heart" (Hebrews 4:12).

KEY IDEA: I study the Bible to know God and his truth and to find direction for my daily life.

GROUP DISCUSSION

As a group, discuss your thoughts and feelings about the following declarations. Which statements are easy to declare with certainty? Which are more challenging? Why?

- I read the Bible daily.
- I regularly study the Bible to find direction for my life.
- I seek to be obedient to God by applying the truth of the Bible to my life.
- I have a good understanding of the contents of the Bible.

Based on your group's dynamics and spiritual maturity, choose two or three questions that will lead to the best discussion about this week's key idea.

1. What are some reasons or motivations a person could possess for studying the Bible? Which of these reasons are most compelling? Why?

2. What obstacles hinder a person from consistently studying the Bible? How can you overcome these challenges?

3. In what ways has the Bible proven a trustworthy map for navigating decisions in your life?

4. Many tools—devotionals, commentaries, reading plans—can help you get the most out of your Bible reading. What are some of the tools that you have found to be helpful?

Read Psalm 119:9-24 and choose one or two questions that will lead to the greatest discussion in your group.

1. What are some ways to "hide God's word in your heart"?

2. In what ways has God's Word been a "lamp for your feet and a light on your path"?

3. The psalmist declares that he loves God's laws and precepts. Why do you think he feels this way?

CASE STUDY

Use the following case study as a model for a real-life situation where you might put this week's key idea into practice.

> Parker is a promising collegian—smart, talented, and charming. Unfortunately, his compulsive and free-spirited nature often leads him to make some foolish decisions. Now that he is entering manhood, the consequences of his actions have become more severe.
>
> Parker grew up going to church but confesses that he has never been committed to reading the Bible for himself. Because he considers you a role model, he asks, "Can you help me? I don't know what I need to do to get my life on track, but I know that what I'm doing isn't working."

Using the following key applications from this session, discuss what you could say or do to help Parker find the direction he is looking for in life.

KEY APPLICATION #1: Keep your heart soft and receptive to God's Word.

KEY APPLICATION #2: Understand the one story of the Bible.

KEY APPLICATION #3: Study God's Word in community.

KEY APPLICATION #4: Memorize God's Word.

CLOSING PRAYER

Close your time together with prayer. Share your prayer requests with one another. Ask God to help you put this week's key idea into practice.

FOR NEXT WEEK

Before your next group meeting, be sure to read through the following personal study and complete the exercises.

VIDEO NOTES ANSWER KEY

how / know, truth, direction / hear / attitudes / heart / receptive / story / community / memorize

PERSONAL STUDY

Last week you examined the practice of prayer. Perhaps you were challenged to seek God's guidance and wisdom by communicating more frequently with him. Before your group meeting, complete the following study. Then take some time to ask God to speak to you.

KEY QUESTION
HOW DO I STUDY GOD'S WORD?

We study God's Word with the intent of letting it guide our lives. In Matthew 4:1–11, we read how Jesus responded to Satan when he was tempted in the wilderness by quoting God's Word. If Jesus battled his archenemy with only the Word of God, we should also make the Bible our "sword" to defeat our enemy. But to *wield* God's Word, we first must *know* God's Word.

Jesus not only authored the Scriptures, but he also came to fulfill and live out every page. Seeing his constant intertwining of the Word into his ministry shows us the vital importance of knowing, understanding, memorizing, and applying the Bible. It is through the Bible that we learn how to think, act, and become like Jesus.

The ancient stories and words of the Scriptures are completely capable of leading us along the right path. But like a trustworthy map or GPS, we must use it for it to be effective.

Making Bible study a key practice in our lives can help us to get to where God wants us to go. So we must read with great eagerness to learn from God's Word and apply it to our lives.

> *When all Israel comes to appear before the LORD your God at the place he will choose, you shall read this law before them in their hearing. Assemble the people—men, women and children, and the foreigners residing in your towns—so they can listen and learn to fear the LORD your God and follow carefully all the words of this law* (Deuteronomy 31:11–12).

> *"Be strong and very courageous. Be careful to obey all the law my servant Moses gave you; do not turn from it to the right or to the left, that you may be successful wherever you go. Keep this Book of the Law always on your lips; meditate on it day and night, so that you may be careful to do everything written in it. Then you will be prosperous and successful"* (Joshua 1:7–8).

> *I seek you with all my heart; do not let me stray from your commands* (Psalm 119:10).

1. What are the benefits of studying God's Word?

   _____

   _____

   _____

   _____

2. Why is God's Word more than just words on a page?

   _____

   _____

   _____

KEY IDEA
I STUDY THE BIBLE TO KNOW GOD AND HIS TRUTH AND FIND DIRECTION FOR MY DAILY LIFE

While your Bible may look like a book that contains paper and ink, Scripture tells us it is alive with God's own breath. His words are not dormant on a page, but active in the lives of those who will consume and apply them.

The believer who attempts to live the Christian life with their Bible gathering dust is like a construction worker trying to build a skyscraper without blueprints. What is the point without the plan? God's Word cuts to the core, acting much like a surgeon's scalpel, exposing what is in our minds for him to do the work in us that only our Creator can do. It gets under our skin, below the surface, to expose our true motives and to reveal the truth to our spirit.

As sinners, we can deceive ourselves, as well as the people around us, with what is truly in our hearts, but the Bible shows us who we actually are, judging our true beliefs. As we read, soak in, and apply its truths, Scripture performs spiritual open-heart surgery. Like a personal counselor, God's Word can go straight to the source of our issues, connecting with and changing our actions, our thoughts, and even our very motives.

For the word of God is alive and active. Sharper than any double-edged sword, it penetrates even to dividing soul and spirit, joints and marrow; it judges the thoughts and attitudes of the heart (Hebrews 4:12).

The law of the LORD is perfect,
refreshing the soul.

The statutes of the LORD are trustworthy,
    making wise the simple.
The precepts of the LORD are right,
    giving joy to the heart.
The commands of the LORD are radiant,
    giving light to the eyes.
The fear of the LORD is pure,
    enduring forever.
The decrees of the LORD are firm,
    and all of them are righteous (Psalm 19:7–9).

Fix these words of mine in your hearts and minds; tie them as symbols on your hands and bind them on your foreheads. Teach them to your children, talking about them when you sit at home and when you walk along the road, when you lie down and when you get up (Deuteronomy 11:18–19).

1. What is the difference between reading God's Word and meditating on it day and night?

2. What experiences have you had studying God's Word on your own? In a community of believers?

KEY APPLICATION
WHAT DIFFERENCE THIS MAKES

We must go to God's Word regularly, because it has the potential to permeate our lives. When we consistently read the pages of the Bible, we declare that we believe what is found there. Bible study strongly reinforces every belief. We discover how to encounter God, how to be saved, who we are in Christ, how to engage in and govern the church; what it means to be a steward, what eternity will be like, how much God cares for and loves his creation—and we receive thousands of precepts, promises, and principles for how to live.

Consider what would happen if for one week you exchanged your phone with your Bible. Anywhere you normally took your phone, you instead took your Bible. Anytime you normally looked at your phone, you instead looked at God's Word. The time you spent calling, texting, and browsing online you instead spent reading Scripture. What difference would this exchange make in your life in just one week? Whose lives would be impacted?

This line of questioning is not intended to trigger guilt in you but rather to inspire you to increase your engagement with the one instrument that can truly change your life and the lives of those around you. As you practice the study of the Bible, God will work his Word in and through your life. The Bible is unlike any other narrative. It is *God's story* . . . chock-full of amazing depth and application. If you are open and receptive to the truths the Bible contains, they will take root and transform your very life.

I have hidden your word in my heart
    that I might not sin against you (Psalm 119:11).

Oh, how I love your law!
  I meditate on it all day long.
Your commands are always with me
  and make me wiser than my enemies. . . .
Your word is a lamp for my feet,
  a light on my path (Psalm 119:97–98, 105).

"But the seed falling on good soil refers to someone who hears the word and understands it. This is the one who produces a crop, yielding a hundred, sixty or thirty times what was sown" (Matthew 13:23).

1. How is the condition of your heart key to understanding God's Word?

   _____

   _____

   _____

2. How does studying God's Word help you know him and his direction for your life?

   _____

   _____

   _____

   _____

EVALUATE

As you conclude this personal study, use a scale of 1–6 to rate how strongly you believe the following statements (1 = no belief at all, 6 = complete confidence):

_____ I read the Bible daily.

_____ I regularly study the Bible to find direction for my life.

_____ I seek to be obedient to God by applying the truth of the Bible to my life.

_____ I have a good understanding of the contents of the Bible.

TAKE ACTION

Memorizing Scripture is a valuable discipline for all believers to exercise. Spend a few minutes each day committing this week's key verse to memory.

KEY VERSE: "For the word of God is alive and active. Sharper than any double-edged sword, it penetrates even to dividing soul and spirit, joints and marrow; it judges the thoughts and attitudes of the heart" (Hebrews 4:12).

Recite this week's key idea out loud. As you do, ask yourself, *Does my life reflect this statement?*

KEY IDEA: I study the Bible to know God and his truth and to find direction for my daily life.

Answer the following questions to help you apply this week's key idea to your own life.

1. How could this practice express itself in your life?

2. What visible attributes can be found in someone who regularly engages in Bible study?

3. What is impeding your ability to consistently engage in Bible study? How can you overcome this obstacle?

4. What step can you take this week to make Bible study a greater part of your daily life?

Session 4

HOW MUCH OF MY LIFE DOES GOD WANT?

You are only able to strive for total surrender in your life through God's wonderful gift of grace. This does not mean you give yourself to him out of some obligation or debt in trade for redemption. Nor does it mean giving up the control because he has overpowered you. Rather, you fully surrender to God out of total desperation and realization of your need for a Savior. As you understand God's gracious provision of mercy through Jesus, you are left with an obvious response of total surrender to God's will. He so captures your heart for today and forever that you are compelled to give up everything to him—based on love, not a sense of duty.

VIDEO TEACHING NOTES

Welcome to session four of *Act Like Jesus*. Spend a few minutes sharing any insights or questions about last week's personal study. Then start the video and use the following outline to record some of the main points. (The answer key is found at the end of the session.)

- Jesus is looking for a "_____ faith" from his followers.

- "Whoever wants to be my disciple must _____ themselves and take up their cross and follow me" (Matthew 16:24).

- **Key Idea:** I _____ my life to God's purposes.

- **Key Question:** How do I cultivate a life of _____ ?

- Every time one of Jesus' disciples was martyred or punished, it only _____ the movement of Christ.

- **Key Verse:** "Therefore, I urge you, brothers and sisters, in view of God's mercy, to _____ your bodies as a living sacrifice, holy and pleasing to God—this is your true and proper worship" (Romans 12:1).

- **(Key Application #1):** Constantly remember the _____ Jesus made for you.

- (Key Application #2): _____ that you are in a no-lose situation.

GETTING STARTED

Begin your discussion by reciting the key verse and key idea together as a group. On your first attempt, use your notes if you need help. On your second attempt, try to state them completely from memory.

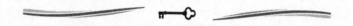

KEY VERSE: "Therefore, I urge you, brothers and sisters, in view of God's mercy, to offer your bodies as a living sacrifice, holy and pleasing to God—this is your true and proper worship" (Romans 12:1).

KEY IDEA: I dedicate my life to God's purposes.

GROUP DISCUSSION

As a group, discuss your thoughts and feelings about the following declarations. Which statements are easy to declare with certainty? Which are more challenging? Why?

- I am living out God's purposes for my life.
- I give up what I want to meet the needs of others.

- I give away things I possess when I am so led by God.
- I serve God through my daily work.

Based on your group's dynamics and spiritual maturity, choose two or three questions that will lead to the best discussion about this week's key idea.

1. Discuss what it takes (mentally, spiritually, and emotionally) to be a person who is completely surrendered to God's purposes.

2. Not everyone is called to vocational ministry. What does total surrender look like for a schoolteacher, plumber, artist, business owner, or you?

3. The disciple Peter learned that total surrender is easier said than done. In what ways can you relate to his story?

4. As ambassadors of Christ, how can acts of sacrifice and surrender reflect God's love to people in your daily life?

_____

_____

_____

_____

_____

Read Daniel 3:1–28 and choose one or two questions that will lead to the greatest discussion in your group.

1. Although the world you live in is drastically different, how can you relate to Shadrach, Meshach, and Abednego?

_____

_____

_____

_____

_____

2. What qualities or virtues, if any, do you see in them that you would like to possess?

_____

_____

_____

_____

_____

3. In this story and many others found in the Bible, people made bold decisions in order to fulfill God's purposes. From where does boldness come? Is it a personality trait? Is it generated through willpower? Is it given by God? Or is it developed over time?

_____

_____

_____

_____

_____

CASE STUDY

Use the following case study as a model for a real-life situation where you might put this week's key idea into practice.

Suzanne's job requires her to travel out of town two or three times a month. For the first time in her life, she is able to put money in the bank rather than live paycheck to paycheck. Unfortunately, her coworkers and her supervisor use these out-of-town trips to feed their wild sides and entertain potential clients. Suzanne feels stuck. She knows the activities on these trips are not pleasing to God, but refusing to participate would most likely cost her her job.

Using the following key applications from this session, discuss what you could say or do to help Suzanne see the importance of doing the right thing.

KEY APPLICATION #1: Constantly remember the sacrifice Jesus made for you.

KEY APPLICATION #2: Remember that you are in a no-lose situation.

CLOSING PRAYER

Close your time together with prayer. Share your prayer requests with one another. Ask God to help you put this week's key idea into practice.

FOR NEXT WEEK

Before your next group meeting, be sure to read through the following personal study and complete the exercises.

VIDEO NOTES ANSWER KEY

cannonball / deny / dedicate / sacrifice / fueled / offer / sacrifice / remember

PERSONAL STUDY

Last week you examined your commitment to the practice of Bible study. Perhaps you learned something about yourself or the Word of God that was new to you. Before your next group meeting, complete the following study. Allow the Scriptures to take root in your heart and then evaluate how much you focus on God in your daily life and give the control completely to him.

KEY QUESTION
HOW DO I CULTIVATE A LIFE OF SACRIFICIAL SERVICE?

Single-mindedness permeates all the key beliefs in acting like Jesus. We recognize that he is God . . . and we are not. We acknowledge that the authority of the Bible should define our priorities. We accept that these priorities must come from Christ. We seek to model the life that he lived in the Gospels—including the practice of daily surrender to God.

Jesus calls those who want to follow him to give up their lives for him (see Matthew 16:24–25). There is thus a high cost involved in living a life of total surrender to Jesus. Furthermore, when he invites us into his work, the time to act is *now*, not later. The day of salvation is always *today*. Delayed obedience is actually disobedience.

When Jesus was healing, performing miracles, and meeting needs, the crowds of people appeared to be all in. But when he made statements about the reality of following him, many decided the cost of total surrender was too much. By the time Jesus was led to the cross, even his closest friends had abandoned him. His final act of total surrender to the Father was completed *alone*. The road walked with Jesus is truly the narrow one (see Matthew 7:13–14).

However, a *genuine* decision to follow and obey God is a decision of *total* surrender. We leave nothing off the negotiation table. After all, God the Father was willing to give up everything for us—offering even the life of his only son. How will we respond to this act?

> *I urge you, brothers and sisters, in view of God's mercy, to offer your bodies as a living sacrifice, holy and pleasing to God—this is your true and proper worship* (Romans 12:1).

> *Then Jesus said to his disciples, "Whoever wants to be my disciple must deny themselves and take up their cross and follow me. For whoever wants to save their life will lose it, but whoever loses their life for me will find it"* (Matthew 16:24–25).

> *But seek first his kingdom and his righteousness, and all these things will be given to you as well (Matthew 6:33).*

1. What distractions often keep you from putting God first?

_____

_____

_____

_____

2. What does it mean to "wholeheartedly" serve God?

_____

_____

_____

KEY IDEA
I DEDICATE MY LIFE TO GOD'S PURPOSES

Jesus made a profound promise to us when he said that "all these things will be given to you" when you choose to "seek first his kingdom and his righteousness" (Matthew 6:33). He promises that if we take care of his business on earth, he will take care of us both here and in eternity. He will bless us when we choose to sacrificially focus on his priorities.

Our culture will try to convince us to focus on own desires—the opposite of what Jesus teaches. A commitment to hand over our lives to an unseen God will not only be unpopular but may also make for some difficult days. We will always get push-back when we choose to go against the grain of the self-centered human nature. We will continually encounter opposition when we choose to dedicate our lives to God's purposes instead of our own.

Yet the only way to truly live out Jesus' calling on our lives is through total surrender. This will result in regular acts of love, not in isolated or rare incidents of self-directed humanitarian effort. Total surrender allows us to love God and live out our calling with our entire being. Our actions become a natural extension of who we are in Christ. We simply put our hand in God's hand and walk with him.

The great challenge for us is to remain faithful to him in this endeavor. Yet when we fail—and we *will* fail at times—we can seek forgiveness and move right back into relationship with God. He is totally committed to us. In turn, he asks for us to be totally committed to him.

> *Jesus replied: "'Love the Lord your God with all your heart and with all your soul and with all your mind.' This is the first and greatest commandment. And the second is like it: 'Love your neighbor as yourself'"* (Matthew 22:37–39).

> *"Anyone who loves their father or mother more than me is not worthy of me; anyone who loves their son or daughter more than me is not worthy of me. Whoever does not take up their cross and follow me is not worthy of me. Whoever finds their life will lose it, and whoever loses their life for my sake will find it"* (Matthew 10:37–39).

> *Let us hold unswervingly to the hope we profess, for he who promised is faithful* (Hebrews 10:23).

1. How is surrendering your life to God an act of worship?

2. How does God help you live the life he desires you to live?

KEY APPLICATION
WHAT DIFFERENCE THIS MAKES

The word *surrender* has been the subject of many classic hymns and continues to be a familiar theme in our churches. Yet the biblical connotation must be continually driven home to remind us and prompt us *daily* to "lay down" our rebellion and self-centered agendas as we "lift our hands" to abdicate control and give all authority to God.

To *surrender* means to give up the battle of the flesh, to give over control of our lives, and to abandon our rights. The battle, control, and rights come from the same place—our sinful nature. Declaring surrender is handing over our hearts fully to Jesus. In light of what God has done to give us life, we choose to offer ourselves back to him as living sacrifices.

Service is the outward display of this new lifestyle. Yet God is no drill sergeant, angrily barking out orders, or some cosmic slave master needing to get the dirty work done. He walks with us as a friend and invites us to work with him as part of his team. As we continually yield to God in surrender, sacrifice, and service, we will be not only a living witness but also a world changer. Our actions will bring us into the company of some of the greatest humans to ever walk the planet—the heroes of our faith (see Hebrews 11:1–12:3).

> [Jesus] said to them all: "Whoever wants to be my disciple must deny themselves and take up their cross daily and follow me. For whoever wants to save their life will lose it, but whoever loses their life for me will save it. What good is it for someone to gain the whole world, and yet lose or forfeit their very self? Whoever is ashamed of me and my words, the Son of Man

*will be ashamed of them when he comes in his glory and in the
glory of the Father and of the holy angels* (Luke 9:23–26).

*However, I consider my life worth nothing to me; my only
aim is to finish the race and complete the task the Lord Jesus
has given me—the task of testifying to the good news of God's
grace* (Acts 20:24).

*Therefore, since we are surrounded by such a great cloud of
witnesses, let us throw off everything that hinders and the
sin that so easily entangles. And let us run with perseverance
the race marked out for us, fixing our eyes on Jesus, the pio-
neer and perfecter of faith. For the joy set before him he endured the cross, scorning its shame, and sat down at the right
hand of the throne of God. Consider him who endured such
opposition from sinners, so that you will not grow weary
and lose heart* (Hebrews 12:1–3).

1. Why is it difficult to abdicate control and give complete
   control of your life to God?

2. How is your understanding of God's love and sacrifice a
   key to living for him?

EVALUATE

As you conclude this personal study, use a scale of 1–6 to rate how strongly you believe the following statements (1 = no belief at all, 6 = complete confidence):

_____ I am living out God's purposes for my life.
_____ I give up what I want to meet the needs of others.
_____ I give away things I possess when I am so led by God.
_____ I serve God through my daily work.

TAKE ACTION

Memorizing Scripture is a valuable discipline for all believers to exercise. Spend a few minutes each day committing this week's key verse to memory.

KEY VERSE: "Therefore, I urge you, brothers and sisters, in view of God's mercy, to offer your bodies as a living sacrifice, holy and pleasing to God—this is your true and proper worship" (Romans 12:1).

Recite this week's key idea out loud. As you do, ask yourself, *Does my life reflect this statement?*

KEY IDEA: I dedicate my life to God's purposes.

Answer the following questions to help you apply this week's key idea to your own life.

1. How would this practice express itself in your life?

2. What visible attributes can be found in someone who is focused on Christ and totally surrendered to God?

3. What is impeding your ability to live singlemindedly and submit your life to God's purposes? How can you overcome this obstacle?

4. What step can you take this week to move closer to a life that is aware of God's involvement and entirely surrendered to him?

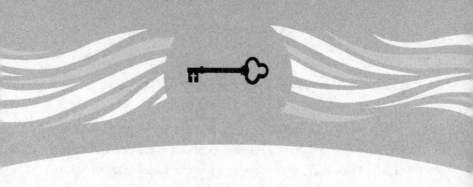

Session 5

HOW DO I DEVELOP HEALTHY RELATIONSHIPS?

WELCOME

We believe the one true God wants to be in a relationship with us for eternity. To make that possible, God provided the way to restore our relationship with him—through the sacrifice of Jesus. All who believe receive a new identity and form a new community called the *church*. The Bible makes it clear through commands, promises, and examples that the Christian life was never intended to be lived alone. Those who have received Christ are now wired through their new spiritual DNA to live in community. We must have a band of believers to walk alongside us, all pointed in the same direction—toward the Father. Only collectively are we the body of Christ. We need each other to help us become like Jesus and consistently model his life.

VIDEO TEACHING NOTES

Welcome to session five of *Act Like Jesus*. Spend a few minutes sharing any insights or questions about last week's personal study. Then start the video and use the following outline to record some of the main points. (The answer key is found at the end of the session.)

- In Genesis 2:18, God said, "It is not good for the man to be _____."

- God is a _____—Father, Son, and Holy Spirit.

- We too were created _____ community and _____ a community.

- **Key Question:** What do I do to develop healthy ____ _____ with others?

- **Key Idea:** I fellowship with Christians to _____ God's purposes in my life, in the lives of others, and in the world.

- **Key Verse:** "All the believers were together and had everything in common. They sold property and possessions to _____ to anyone who had need. Every day they continued to _____ together in the temple courts. They broke bread in their homes and _____ together with glad and sincere hearts, praising God and enjoying the favor of all the people. And the Lord added to their number daily those who were being saved" (Acts 2:44–47).

- **(Key Application #1)**: Fellowship with other believers to keep your relationship with _____ _____ strong.

- **(Key Application #2)**: Fellowship with other believers to keep your relationships with _____ _____ strong.

- **(Key Application #3)**: Fellowship with other believers to _____ God's will on earth.

GETTING STARTED

Begin your discussion by reciting the key verse and key idea together as a group. On your first attempt, use your notes if you need help. On your second attempt, try to state them completely from memory.

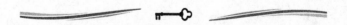

KEY VERSE: "All the believers were together and had everything in common. They sold property and possessions to give to anyone who had need. Every day they continued to meet together in the temple courts. They broke bread in their homes and ate together with glad and sincere hearts, praising God and enjoying the favor of all the people. And the Lord added to their number daily those who were being saved" (Acts 2:44–47).

KEY IDEA: I fellowship with Christians to accomplish God's purposes in my life, in the lives of others, and in the world.

GROUP DISCUSSION

As a group, discuss your thoughts and feelings about the following declarations. Which statements are easy to declare with certainty? Which are more challenging? Why?

- I have close relationships with other Christians who have influence on my life's direction.
- I participate in a group of Christians who really know me and support me.
- I allow other Christians to hold me accountable for my actions.
- I daily pray for and support other Christians.

Based on your group's dynamics and spiritual maturity, choose two or three questions that will lead to the best discussion about this week's key idea.

1. In what ways is it "not good for [a person] to be alone"?

   _____

   _____

   _____

   _____

2. In a world where people are becoming more isolated and self-centered, what can be done to nurture a more vibrant others-focused community?

   _____

   _____

   _____

   _____

3. What is an adversary of biblical community? In other words, what in your life or culture impedes the success of healthy, attractive, faith-based community?

   _____

   _____

   _____

   _____

4. What simple steps could this group take to enhance and/ or develop more connection with God, each other, and non-believers?

   _____

   _____

   _____

   _____

Read Acts 2:42–47 and choose one or two questions that will lead to the greatest discussion in your group.

1. In what ways has your church experience been similar to what you just read? How has it been different?

2. Is the type of community you just read about possible today? Why or why not?

3. If community is something we desperately need, why do you think so many people of faith today are content to live lifestyles of isolation?

CASE STUDY

Use the following case study as a model for a real-life situation where you might put this week's key idea into practice.

Lauren began to follow Christ as a teenager after a close friend invited her to a church summer camp. Not growing up in a religious family made her feel far behind in her faith. So she immediately began to read every Bible study she could find. Lauren's faith soared as she learned more about herself and the character of God. Ten years have passed, and she still reads her Bible daily and attends services at her church. But she feels as if something is missing . . . as if she has hit a spiritual plateau and doesn't know what to do to change it.

Using the following key applications from this session, discuss what you could say or do to help Lauren.

KEY APPLICATION #1: Fellowship with other believers to keep your relationship with God strong.

KEY APPLICATION #2: Fellowship with other believers to keep your relationships with others strong.

KEY APPLICATION #3: Fellowship with other believers to accomplish God's will on earth.

CLOSING PRAYER

Close your time together with prayer. Share your prayer requests with one another. Ask God to help you put this week's key idea into practice.

FOR NEXT WEEK

Before your next group meeting, be sure to read through the following personal study and complete the exercises.

VIDEO NOTES ANSWER KEY

alone / community / for, as / relationships / accomplish / give, meet, ate / God / others / accomplish

PERSONAL STUDY

Last week you examined the practice of total surrender. Perhaps you were challenged to jump in "cannonball" style and actively lay down your life for God's purposes. Before your next group meeting, complete the following study. Allow some time for the Scriptures to soak in as you evaluate your personal practice of biblical community.

KEY QUESTION

HOW DO I DEVELOP HEALTHY RELATIONSHIPS WITH OTHERS?

Have you ever thought about the way Jesus recruited his disciples? He is God, so he could have easily walked down the beach and assembled an army of 12,000 men to overthrow the government. He could have called 1,200 and together given them amazing powers. But he did nothing of the sort. In fact, he didn't even call 120. Essentially, Jesus formed the first "small group," as they are called in the church today. He launched his ministry with twelve men. He put together a tiny community of diverse and, frankly, mostly unimpressive followers.

Why did Jesus take this approach? The reason is because he wasn't planning a coup or forming a cult. Rather, he was building a *community*. He didn't call those he chose based on their résumé, IQ, or brawn. Yet the fact that his original small group formed the church that still thrives today reveals that he chose wisely. He prepared this body of believers to carry out his work—a work that swept through the known world after his ascension into heaven.

Biblical community is essential to the Christian life and is a vital aspect of the church. God intended for us to have rich, meaningful, life-giving relationships with each other. He desires for us to have relationships energized and motivated by his presence among us. As we engage in this new family under God's leadership, we not only achieve his purposes in our lives, in the lives of others, and in the world, but we also reinforce our belief in God and his church.

> *Two are better than one,*
> > *because they have a good return for their labor:*
> *If either of them falls down,*
> > *one can help the other up.*
> *But pity anyone who falls*
> > *and has no one to help them up.*
> *Also, if two lie down together, they will keep warm.*
> > *But how can one keep warm alone?*
> *Though one may be overpowered,*
> > *two can defend themselves.*
> *A cord of three strands is not quickly broken*
> (Ecclesiastes 4:9–12).

> *You are no longer foreigners and strangers, but fellow citizens with God's people and also members of his household, built on the foundation of the apostles and prophets, with Christ Jesus himself as the chief cornerstone. In him the whole building is joined together and rises to become a holy temple in the Lord. And in him you too are being built*

together to become a dwelling in which God lives by his Spirit (Ephesians 2:19–22).

1. Why is biblical community important?

_____

_____

_____

_____

2. How does faith in Christ Jesus bind people together?

_____

_____

_____

_____

KEY IDEA

I FELLOWSHIP WITH CHRISTIANS TO ACCOMPLISH GOD'S PURPOSES IN MY LIFE, IN THE LIFE OF OTHERS, AND IN THE WORLD

To properly define biblical community, we need look no further than the last few syllables in the word—*unity*. This is both the point and practice of the concept of community. Our unity is an example to the world that is watching how we treat each other. It is the strength by which we reach out to this watching world and display God's love for them.

Christ's vision is that we would become an integral part of his grand body of believers. He desires us to usher in his kingdom around the globe by being grafted into the lives of a local body and make a difference right where we are. The ministry we do for a neighbor truly does impact the world as we join in obeying Christ. It is a "one for all, and all for one" battle cry.

Of course, in order to sustain such life-giving community, God must be at the center of it. Through the Holy Spirit, the presence of God actually dwells in and among believers. God's presence in our hearts magnifies our potential for vibrant community. The practice of biblical community reinforces both our belief in our identity in Christ individually and our belief in the church to—*together*—be his hands and feet to the world.

> *I urge you to live a life worthy of the calling you have received. Be completely humble and gentle; be patient, bearing with one another in love. Make every effort to keep the unity of the Spirit through the bond of peace. There is one body and one Spirit, just as you were called to one hope when you were called; one Lord, one faith, one baptism; one God and Father of all, who is over all and through all and in all* (Ephesians 4:1–6).

> *They devoted themselves to the apostles' teaching and to fellowship, to the breaking of bread and to prayer. Everyone was filled with awe at the many wonders and signs performed by the apostles. All the believers were together and had everything in common. They sold property and possessions to give to anyone who had need. Every day they continued to meet together in the temple courts. They broke bread in their homes and ate together with glad and sincere hearts, praising God and enjoying the favor of all the people. And the Lord added to their number daily those who were being saved* (Acts 2:42–47).

Finally, all of you, be like-minded, be sympathetic, love one another, be compassionate and humble (1 Peter 3:8).

1. What words would you use to describe your community of believers?

   _____

   _____

   _____

2. Who in your community of believers inspires you to serve God and accomplish his purposes?

   _____

   _____

   _____

   _____

KEY APPLICATION
WHAT DIFFERENCE THIS MAKES

Who we spend our time with has an impact on our lives. Fellowship with other believers will keep our relationship with *God* strong. Nothing will hold us accountable and encourage us to follow Jesus quite like other Christ-followers. In the same way, fellowship with other believers will also keep our relationships with *others* strong. Biblical community is the optimum way to keep our horizontal relationships on the right and righteous path.

As we build community within the church, we build a foundation on which we can accomplish God's will on earth.

As we minister and reach out to those in the world, our community of faith allows us to stay tethered to Christ so we will succeed. There are days we desperately just need a good hug to keep going . . . and other days when we need a swift kick in the pants to get back to where we should be. Friends who love God and love us for who we are know exactly when and how to do the right thing for us.

Biblical community is the glue holding us together. It enables us to grow in favor with God and keep our relationships right with others. Even a small gathering of believers has power. In truth, it doesn't take hundreds of people to make a difference for God. Jesus said it just takes a few who are committed to gathering around a common purpose. Whatever the composition of the group, biblical community engages all its members to use their gifts, resources, and time in unison to accomplish a task important to the plan of God.

> And let us consider how we may spur one another on toward love and good deeds, not giving up meeting together, as some are in the habit of doing, but encouraging one another—and all the more as you see the Day approaching (Hebrews 10:24).

> Wounds from a friend can be trusted, but an enemy multiplies kisses (Proverbs 27:6).

> For where two or three gather in my name, there am I with them (Matthew 18:20).

> He died for us so that, whether we are awake or asleep, we may live together with him. Therefore encourage one

another and build each other up, just as in fact you are doing (1 Thessalonians 5:10–11).

1. How can a community of believers grow their relationship with God?

   _____

   _____

   _____

   _____

2. How can a community of believers serve God in the world effectively?

   _____

   _____

   _____

   _____

EVALUATE

As you conclude this personal study, use a scale of 1–6 to rate how strongly you believe the following statements (1 = no belief at all, 6 = complete confidence):

_____ I have close relationships with other Christians who have influence on my life's direction.

_____ I participate in a group of Christians who really know me and support me.

_____ I allow other Christians to hold me accountable for my actions.

_____ I daily pray for and support other Christians.

TAKE ACTION

Memorizing Scripture is a valuable discipline for all believers to exercise. Spend a few minutes each day committing this week's key verse to memory.

KEY VERSE: "All the believers were together and had everything in common. They sold property and possessions to give to anyone who had need. Every day they continued to meet together in the temple courts. They broke bread in their homes and ate together with glad and sincere hearts, praising God and enjoying the favor of all the people. And the Lord added to their number daily those who were being saved" (Acts 2:44–47).

Recite this week's key idea out loud. As you do, ask yourself, _Does my life reflect this statement?_

KEY IDEA: I fellowship with Christians to accomplish God's purposes in my life, in the lives of others, and in the world.

Answer the following questions to help you apply this week's key idea to your own life.

1. How would this practice express itself in your life?

   _____

   _____

   _____

   _____

2. What visible attributes can be found in someone who practices biblical community?

   _____

   _____

   _____

   _____

3. What is impeding your ability to experience biblical community? How can you overcome this obstacle?

   _____

   _____

   _____

   _____

   _____

4. What step can you take this week to develop biblical community?

   _____

   _____

   _____

   _____

Session 6

WHAT SPIRITUAL GIFTS HAS GOD GIVEN TO ME?

When God formed us in the womb, he molded and shaped our personality and our abilities. He gave us certain talents to use for our personal satisfaction and for the benefit of the world. But when we made the decision to embrace God's offer of salvation . . . something else happened in our lives. The Bible is clear that at this moment, the Holy Spirit came to indwell our lives and deposited a spiritual gift (or gifts) within us. God offered these gifts out of his treasury of righteous qualities. We did not have to ask him—he provided them to us freely. God has also now repurposed the innate talents he created in us. He wants to use those innate talents alongside the spiritual gifts he has provided for a high and eternal purpose.

VIDEO TEACHING NOTES

Welcome to session six of *Act Like Jesus*. Spend a few minutes sharing any insights or questions about last week's personal study. Then start the video and use the following outline to record some of the main points. (The answer key is found at the end of the session.)

- **Key Question**: What gifts and skills has God given me to _____ others?

- **Key Verse**: "For just as each of us has one body with many members, and these members do not all have the same function, so in Christ we, though many, form one body, and each member _____ _____ to all the others. We have different gifts, according to the grace given to each of us" (Romans 12:4–6).

- **Key Idea**: I know my spiritual gifts and _____ them to fulfill God's purposes.

- **(Key Application #1)**: As a community, help each other _____ what gift God has given to each of you.

- **(Key Application #2)**: Know and _____ _____ the gifts of the people God has placed around you.

- **(Key Application #3)**: _____ your gift.

- **(Key Application #4):** Acknowledge and give God the _____ for your gift.

GETTING STARTED

Begin your discussion by reciting the key verse and key idea together as a group. On your first attempt, use your notes if you need help. On your second attempt, try to state them completely from memory.

KEY VERSE: "For just as each of us has one body with many members, and these members do not all have the same function, so in Christ we, though many, form one body, and each member belongs to all the others. We have different gifts, according to the grace given to each of us" (Romans 12:4–6).

KEY IDEA: I know my spiritual gifts and use them to fulfill God's purposes.

GROUP DISCUSSION

As a group, discuss your thoughts and feelings about the following declarations. Which statements are easy to declare with certainty? Which are more challenging? Why?

- I know my spiritual gift(s).
- I regularly use my spiritual gift(s) in ministry to accomplish God's purposes.
- I value the spiritual gifts of others to accomplish God's purposes.
- Others recognize and affirm my spiritual gift(s) and support my use of them.

Based on your group's dynamics and spiritual maturity, choose two or three questions that will lead to the best discussion about this week's key idea.

1. What are some specific ways you see members of your group using their spiritual gifts?

2. Which parts of your spiritual community are thriving? Which parts are hurting or nonexistent? What steps can the group take to strengthen the body of Christ?

3. If some in the group are unsure of their roles in the body of Christ, how would you advise them to discover their spiritual giftedness?

4. Some gifts get more attention than others, which can cause pride and jealousy within the body of Christ. How can your group safeguard against this attitude?

_____

_____

_____

Read 1 Corinthians 12:4–31 and choose one or two questions that will lead to the best discussion in your group.

1. What role does your spiritual gift play in the redemption and restoration of broken people and a broken world?

_____

_____

2. Paul notes there are parts of the human body that are not visible but are incredibly important in order for the body to function properly. Which gifts within the body of Christ are rarely recognized yet vital to the success of the church's mission?

_____

_____

_____

_____

3. Why is it critical to use your gifts with an attitude of love?

_____

_____

_____

CASE STUDY

Use the following case study as a model for a real-life situation where you might put this week's key idea into practice.

> Danny is frustrated. After giving his life to Christ five years ago, he has desperately tried to share the good news with as many people as possible. He has taught Bible studies at work, church, and in his neighborhood, but without the success he had hoped to achieve. Initially he would get a good turnout, but people would gradually lose interest.
>
> A couple of months ago, a coworker invited Danny to a Bible study on Thursdays during their lunch hour. It started out as a small group, but within a few weeks the break room at the company was packed. Danny knew that he should be excited, but he was just mad. Why was this coworker having so much success, when Danny hadn't? He couldn't understand what he was doing wrong.

Using the following key applications from this session, discuss what you could say or do to help Danny find the answers to his frustrations.

KEY APPLICATION #1: As a community, help each other discover what gift God has given to each of you.

KEY APPLICATION #2: Know and celebrate the gifts of the people God has placed around you.

KEY APPLICATION #3: Use your gift.

KEY APPLICATION #4: Acknowledge and give God the credit for your gift.

CLOSING PRAYER

Close your time together with prayer. Share your prayer requests with one another. Ask God to help you put this week's key idea into practice.

FOR NEXT WEEK

Before your next group meeting, be sure to read through the following personal study and complete the exercises.

VIDEO NOTES ANSWER KEY

serve / belongs / use / discover / celebrate / use / credit

PERSONAL STUDY

Last week, you examined the practice of biblical community. Perhaps you discovered that community is not just nice to participate in but is also necessary for a full and healthy lifestyle. Before your next group meeting, complete the following study. Allow the Scripture to take root in your heart as you consider the spiritual gift (or gifts) that God has given to you.

KEY QUESTION
WHAT GIFTS AND ABILITIES HAS GOD GIVEN ME TO SERVE OTHERS?

God instills in us the resources that are needed to accomplish his purposes. This includes not only the work of the pastor who leads a flock at church but also the work of a builder who swings a hammer at a construction site. The Bible is clear that *all* believers have at least one spiritual gift.

So, how can you identify your gift(s) so you can best use them? A simple method is to consider how you would react to different situations where your help might be needed. Do you immediately take charge? Do you like to organize and oversee details? Do you focus on the needs of people? Do you have a heart to serve and support those who are sacrificing time and energy to address a need? Do you have the ability to gather information to help a cause? Are you glad to do whatever needs to be done? The role you see yourself taking can reveal a great deal about the spiritual gift(s) that God has given to you.

As you do so, remember your gift(s) have not been given for your personal benefit but to serve in concert with other members of the body of Christ. It is up to each person to acknowledge and use his or her gift(s) for God's intended purposes. Then, collectively, the community must decide to work together in *unity*. God wants to redeem this broken world, and he has chosen to use us—the church—to do it. When this happens, the power of the Holy Spirit is displayed, and amazing things are accomplished in this world.

> *"The Advocate, the Holy Spirit, whom the Father will send in my name, will teach you all things and will remind you of everything I have said to you. Peace I leave with you; my peace I give you. I do not give to you as the world gives. Do not let your hearts be troubled and do not be afraid"* (John 14:26–27).

> *For just as each of us has one body with many members, and these members do not all have the same function, so in Christ we, though many, form one body, and each member belongs to all the others. We have different gifts, according to the grace given to each of us* (Romans 12:4–6).

> *This salvation, which was first announced by the Lord, was confirmed to us by those who heard him. God also testified to it by signs, wonders and various miracles, and by gifts of the Holy Spirit distributed according to his will* (Hebrews 2:3–4).

1. How does the Bible indicate that spiritual gifts are distributed to believers in Christ?

_____

_____

_____

_____

2. How would you describe the difference between a spiritual gift and a talent or ability?

_____

_____

_____

_____

KEY IDEA
I KNOW MY SPIRITUAL GIFTS AND USE THEM TO FULFILL GOD'S PURPOSES

God's intention is for us to meet needs of people on earth by working together for his glory. When you became a member of the body of Christ, you joined a community of believers who are under the authority and guidance of God himself. The contribution of your gift(s) will accomplish his purposes for the advancement of the kingdom.

Your spiritual gift(s) are thus to be practiced out of a heart of grace, humility, and faith (see Romans 12:3). You are commissioned to discover what God has gifted you to do and to use your gift(s) for his glory, for the benefit of the body of

Christ, and to serve needs in the world. Your spiritual gift(s) should be used for the good of others, multiplying the blessing as you share them according to God's purposes.

Basically, the goal is to discover your gift and then find ways to give it away! Just as a piston engine requires pure gasoline to run smoothly, your gifts must be fueled with loving intentions. Spiritual gifts that are powered by selfish ambition and pride will only sputter and fail. But gifts fueled with love will run on and on as God's kingdom grows.

We have different gifts, according to the grace given to each of us. If your gift is prophesying, then prophesy in accordance with your faith; if it is serving, then serve; if it is teaching, then teach; if it is to encourage, then give encouragement; if it is giving, then give generously; if it is to lead, do it diligently; if it is to show mercy, do it cheerfully (Romans 12:6–8).

There are different kinds of gifts, but the same Spirit distributes them. There are different kinds of service, but the same Lord. There are different kinds of working, but in all of them and in everyone it is the same God at work. Now to each one the manifestation of the Spirit is given for the common good (1 Corinthians 12:4–7).

If I speak in the tongues of men or of angels, but do not have love, I am only a resounding gong or a clanging cymbal. If I have the gift of prophecy and can fathom all mysteries and all knowledge, and if I have a faith that can move mountains, but do not have love, I am nothing. If I give all I possess to the poor and give over my body to hardship that I may boast, but do not have love, I gain nothing (1 Corinthians 13:1–3).

1. What spiritual gifts do you believe you possess?

   _____

   _____

   _____

   _____

2. Why is the attitude in which you use your spiritual gifts important?

   _____

   _____

   _____

   _____

KEY APPLICATION
WHAT DIFFERENCE THIS MAKES

As we consider spiritual gifts, we have to ask why God would only give us one or two of them rather than giving every gift to all. He certainly *could* do such a thing. The answer connects back to biblical community. God wants us to rely on each other and cooperate with each other. Our limitations create a need for us to work together in sharing our gifts to accomplish a common goal. It also enables us to stay humble, for we know we cannot reach the world alone.

As a hurting world watches us cooperate and move in unison to meet needs, they will want to experience the life-changing power of shunning the "every man for himself" attitude and embracing the "every soul matters" mission of Jesus. The Holy Spirit will direct our efforts in this as we use our gift(s) to model God's love for the world. He knows what is needed, when it is needed, and where it is needed. Our task is to listen to him and obey his instructions. This ongoing process will continually strengthen and hone our connection to the Father.

The Creator has given you a divine gift . . . and he wants you to use it to change the world! So, seek him in prayer and ask him to reveal those gifts to you. As you do, you will find that God will produce supernatural results far above what you could ask for or even imagine.

> *Each of you should use whatever gift you have received to serve others, as faithful stewards of God's grace in its various forms. If anyone speaks, they should do so as one who speaks the very words of God. If anyone serves, they should do so with the strength God provides, so that in all things God may be praised through Jesus Christ. To him be the glory and the power for ever and ever. Amen* (1 Peter 4:10–11).

> *Speaking the truth in love, we will grow to become in every respect the mature body of him who is the head, that is, Christ. From him the whole body, joined and held together by every supporting ligament, grows and builds itself up in love, as each part does its work* (Ephesians 4:15–16).

> *But one thing I do: forgetting what is behind and straining toward what is ahead, I press on toward the goal to win the prize for which God has called me heavenward in Christ Jesus* (Philippians 3:13–14).

1. Why is it important for every follower of Jesus to use his or her gifts?

   _____

   _____

   _____

   _____

2. What are some of the consequences of *not* using your spiritual gift(s)?

   _____

   _____

   _____

   _____

   _____

EVALUATE

As you conclude this personal study, use a scale of 1–6 to rate how strongly you believe the following statements (1 = no belief at all, 6 = complete confidence):

____ I know my spiritual gift(s).

____ I regularly use my spiritual gift(s) in ministry to accomplish God's purposes.

____ I value the spiritual gifts of others to accomplish God's purposes.

____ Others recognize and affirm my spiritual gift(s) and support my use of them.

TAKE ACTION

Memorizing Scripture is a valuable discipline for all believers to exercise. Spend a few minutes each day committing this week's key verse to memory.

KEY VERSE: "For just as each of us has one body with many members, and these members do not all have the same function, so in Christ we, though many, form one body, and each member belongs to all the others. We have different gifts, according to the grace given to each of us" (Romans 12:4-6).

Recite this week's key idea out loud. As you do, ask yourself, *Does my life reflect this statement?*

KEY IDEA: I know my spiritual gifts and use them to fulfill God's purposes.

Answer the following questions to help you apply this week's key idea to your own life.

1. How would this practice express itself in your life?

2. What visible attributes can be found in someone who uses his or her spiritual gifts?

3. What is impeding your ability to know and use your spiritual gifts? How can you overcome this obstacle?

4. What step can you take this week to discover or better use your spiritual gifts?

Session 7

HOW DO I USE MY MONEY TO SERVE GOD?

WELCOME

For children, there is a difference between "have to" and "get to." "You *have* to go to the doctor for a shot." "You *get* to go out for ice cream." Early on, we learn to divide activities we perceive to be fun or boring, good or bad, positive or negative. As adults, we still experience plenty of "have to" and "get to" moments. But these can move from one to the other depending on the person and the circumstances. For instance, one person finds great joy in giving to support the gospel ministry, while another views it as a heavy burden. One person sees time spent serving as time well spent, while another sees time as something to conserve and only use for personal reasons. What marks the difference in the two perspectives? What draws the line between joy and drudgery or delineates the boundary between generosity and greed? How do we best use the resources of time and money that we have been given?

VIDEO TEACHING NOTES

Welcome to session seven of *Act Like Jesus*. Spend a few minutes sharing any insights or questions about last week's personal study. Then start the video and use the following outline to record some of the main points. (The answer key is found at the end of the session.)

- **Key Question**: How do I best use my _____ to serve God and others?

- **Key Idea**: I give my resources to _____ God's purposes.

- **Key Verse**: "But since you excel in everything—in faith, in speech, in knowledge, in complete earnestness and in the love we have kindled in you—see that you also excel in this grace of _____ " (2 Corinthians 8:7).

- **(Key Application #1)**: Your willingness comes from a heart _____ by God's purposes.

- **(Key Application #2)**: Resources go _____ _____ money.

- **(Key Application #3)**: Giving to others _____ _____ your intimacy with Christ.

GETTING STARTED

Begin your discussion by reciting the key verse and key idea together as a group. On your first attempt, use your notes if you need help. On your second attempt, try to state them completely from memory.

KEY VERSE: "But since you excel in everything—in faith, in speech, in knowledge, in complete earnestness and in the love we have kindled in you—see that you also excel in this grace of giving" (2 Corinthians 8:7).

KEY IDEA: I give my resources to fulfill God's purposes.

GROUP DISCUSSION

As a group, discuss your thoughts and feelings about the following declarations. Which statements are easy to declare with certainty? Which are more challenging? Why?

- I give away 10 percent or more of my income to God's work.
- I regularly give money to serve and help others.
- My first priority in spending is to support God's work.

- My spending habits do not keep me from giving what I feel I should give to God.

Based on your group's dynamics and spiritual maturity, choose two or three questions that will lead to the best discussion about this week's key idea.

1. Fire can be beneficial but, if not used properly, also terribly dangerous. How are material resources similar?

2. In what ways can money give you a false sense of security, satisfaction, and safety?

3. Why do you think God is more concerned about the intentions of the giver than the size of the gift?

4. What circumstances in your life provide opportunities to give away some of your resources for God's purposes?

_____

_____

_____

_____

_____

Read Proverbs 11:24–25, 28 and Ecclesiastes 5:10–20 and choose one to two questions that will lead to the greatest discussion in your group.

1. What truths can be found in the passages that you just read together?

_____

_____

_____

_____

2. King Solomon was one of the wealthiest men to ever walk the earth. In what ways, if any, are you surprised by his comments on wealth and money? Which of his comments do you think are the most insightful?

_____

_____

_____

_____

_____

3. If you could sum up Solomon's advice in one or two sentences, what would you say?

_____

_____

_____

_____

CASE STUDY

Use the following case study as a model for a real-life situation where you might put this week's key idea into practice.

> Karen and Ben were married for twenty-eight years before a yearlong battle with cancer took him home to be with Jesus. Left with an abundance of time, money, and a four-bedroom house, Karen ponders what she should do with all of her and Ben's belongings.

Using the following key applications from this session, what could you say or do to help Karen find the direction that she is seeking?

KEY APPLICATION #1: Your willingness comes from a heart moved by God's purposes.

KEY APPLICATION #2: Resources go beyond money.

KEY APPLICATION #3: Giving to others strengthens your intimacy with Christ.

CLOSING PRAYER

Close your time together with prayer. Share your prayer requests with one another. Ask God to help you put this week's key idea into practice.

FOR NEXT WEEK

Before your next group meeting, be sure to read through the following personal study and complete the exercises.

VIDEO NOTES ANSWER KEY

resources / fulfill / giving / moved / beyond / strengthens

PERSONAL STUDY

Last week you examined the practice of spiritual gifts. Perhaps you learned that God has empowered us to work together—as one body—for his purposes. Isn't that incredible! Before your next group meeting, complete the following study. Allow God's Word to shape your thoughts and feelings as it relates to your use of time and your relationship with money.

KEY QUESTION

HOW DO I BEST USE MY RESOURCES TO SERVE GOD AND OTHERS?

The Bible provides many passages about our use of time. Paul's words in Colossians 3:17 are particularly helpful in reminding us that our daily schedule should look much different now than it did before our salvation: "Whatever you do, whether in word or deed, do it all in the name of the Lord Jesus, giving thanks to God the Father through him."

Likewise, the Bible has much to say about how we use our money. Of Jesus' thirty-eight parables, sixteen of them deal with how to handle possessions. References in the Gospels to using personal resources are greater than references to topics such as faith and prayer. Jesus knew that our hearts are focused on money. His teaching continually directs us toward using all we have—including our money and our possessions—to love him and love others.

Believe is an action verb. Whatever we believe in our hearts will be expressed in the way we live. Whenever we act on our belief in God by offering our time and resources to serve him—even if our hearts are not totally committed—it drives our beliefs from our heads to our hearts. Acting on our beliefs is a step of faith. As we act in faith, God replenishes and renews us, helping us manage our time and resources according to his design.

> *"Do not store up for yourselves treasures on earth, where moths and vermin destroy, and where thieves break in and steal. But store up for yourselves treasures in heaven, where moths and vermin do not destroy, and where thieves do not break in and steal. For where your treasure is, there your heart will be also* (Matthew 6:19–21).

> *Whatever you do, whether in word or deed, do it all in the name of the Lord Jesus, giving thanks to God the Father through him* (Colossians 3:17).

> *Since you excel in everything—in faith, in speech, in knowledge, in complete earnestness and in the love we have kindled in you—see that you also excel in this grace of giving* (2 Corinthians 8:7).

1. What drives people's choices concerning using their money, possessions, and time?

   _____

   _____

   _____

   _____

2. How can your attitude toward money illustrate your relationship with Jesus?

KEY IDEA
I GIVE MY RESOURCES TO FULFILL GOD'S PURPOSES

God's grace should move us to feel that we are *privileged* to give rather than we are *required* to give. As devoted followers of Christ, our daily prayer becomes, "Lord, how do you want me to use all the resources you have entrusted to me?" This practice is directly tied to the belief of stewardship—that everything we are and everything we own already belongs to God. Therein lies our dividing line. Do we perceive our money, our resources, to be God's—or ours?

What keeps many Christians from giving isn't a lack of desire but an abundance of personal debt. All too often, this debt comes not from medical bills due to unforeseen illnesses or unavoidable tragedies as from intentional choices to accumulate things. This places an unbearable burden on people and prevents them from receiving the blessings of giving to God and his kingdom. While many Christians today would say they love God and desire to serve him, their devotion must go to "serving" the payments demanded each month.

Before we take on this voluntary debt, we need to recognize that we are *stewards* of God's resources and that he has called us to use a portion of our money to further his purposes. Money will never save anyone's soul, but funds are needed to support ministries that reach people with the gospel. If we truly believe the only thing that will matter in heaven is what we have done for Christ here on earth, then the vast majority of the money that goes through our hands won't count for much—except for what has been given to build Christ's kingdom.

> *Yours, LORD, is the greatness and the power*
> *and the glory and the majesty and the splendor,*
> *for everything in heaven and earth is yours.*
> *Yours, LORD, is the kingdom;*
> *you are exalted as head over all* (1 Chronicles 29:11).

> *"No one can serve two masters. Either you will hate the one and love the other, or you will be devoted to the one and despise the other. You cannot serve both God and money"* (Matthew 6:24).

> *Each of you should give what you have decided in your heart to give, not reluctantly or under compulsion, for God loves a cheerful giver. And God is able to bless you abundantly, so that in all things at all times, having all that you need, you will abound in every good work* (2 Corinthians 9:7–8).

1. Why is a willing heart in giving of your time and your resources so important to God?

_____

_____

_____

2. What are some ways that God uses resources through the giving of willing hearts?

_____

_____

_____

_____

KEY APPLICATION
WHAT DIFFERENCE THIS MAKES

Here is an interesting challenge. Look at the last thirty days of your expenses and identify patterns for how you are spending your money. Then look at your calendar to see how you have used your time. As you do this, ask yourself, "Am I using the resources God has given me to accomplish his purposes?" If the answer is yes, thank God for his wisdom and provision. But if the answer is no . . . it's time to look at the attitude of your heart.

The good news is that God, who is faithful and just, will forgive you and help you transform how you use your time and resources. But it all starts with the heart. There's a decision to make. Who will you serve? Remember, we are *in* the world but not *of* it. So, whether it takes a few months or a few years, seek to get your house in order. God has the unique ability to multiply what his people offer him and bless that to which he is given access.

Giving away your money and resources will not only be beneficial for the recipients but also for you. When you make giving a regular habit, you honor God and keep greed at bay. When you give from a pure heart—totally committed to Christ who gave everything for you—you participate in building God's kingdom and fulfilling God's purposes for your life.

> *One person gives freely, yet gains even more;*
>> *another withholds unduly, but comes to poverty.*
> *A generous person will prosper;*
>> *whoever refreshes others will be refreshed*
> (Proverbs 11:24–25).

> *"So when you give to the needy, do not announce it with trumpets, as the hypocrites do in the synagogues and on the streets, to be honored by others. Truly I tell you, they have received their reward in full. But when you give to the needy, do not let your left hand know what your right hand is doing, so that your giving may be in secret. Then your Father, who sees what is done in secret, will reward you"* (Matthew 6:2–4).

> *I have been crucified with Christ and I no longer live, but Christ lives in me. The life I now live in the body, I live by faith in the Son of God, who loved me and gave himself for me* (Galatians 2:20).

1. How can putting God at the center of your finances impact your relationship with God?

_____

_____

_____

_____

_____

_____

2. What are the eternal benefits of using your time and money for God's purposes?

_____

_____

_____

_____

_____

_____

EVALUATE

As you conclude this personal study, use a scale of 1–6 to rate how strongly you believe the following statements (1 = no belief at all, 6 = complete confidence):

_____ I give away 10 percent or more of my income to God's work.

_____ I regularly give money to serve and help others.

_____ My first priority in spending is to support God's work.

_____ My spending habits do not keep me from giving what I feel I should give to God.

TAKE ACTION

Memorizing Scripture is a valuable discipline for all believers to exercise. Spend a few minutes each day committing this week's key verse to memory.

KEY VERSE: "But since you excel in everything—in faith, in speech, in knowledge, in complete earnestness and in the love we have kindled in you—see that you also excel in this grace of giving" (2 Corinthians 8:7).

Recite this week's key idea out loud. As you do, ask yourself, *Does my life reflect this statement?*

KEY IDEA: I give my resources to fulfill God's purposes.

Answer the following questions to help you apply this week's key idea to your own life.

1. How would this practice express itself in your life?

   _____

   _____

   _____

2. What visible attributes can be found in someone who regularly gives away his or her time and money for God's purposes?

   _____

   _____

   _____

3. What is impeding your ability to offer your time and money to God and others? How can you overcome this obstacle?

_____

_____

_____

_____

4. What step can you take this week to make this practice a consistent part of your life?

_____

_____

_____

_____

Session 8

HOW DO I COMMUNICATE MY FAITH?

For a majority of Christians—particularly in our politically correct culture—talking with a nonbeliever about a relationship with Jesus seems an intimidating task. Weather. Fashion. Sports. Current events. All good. But *Jesus*? Not so much. Putting us on the defensive is an effective strategy that Satan uses to keep us from sharing our faith. But we need to remember that God has purposed the church to be the primary ambassador of spreading the good news of what Jesus did for us to the world. We also need to remember that God can open doors and orchestrate amazing things to happen when we take the risk to reach out!

VIDEO TEACHING NOTES

Welcome to session eight of *Act Like Jesus*. Spend a few minutes sharing any insights or questions about last week's personal study. Then start the video and use the following outline to record some of the main points. (The answer key is found at the end of the session.)

- **Key Question**: How do I share my _____ with those who don't know God?

- **Key Idea**: I _____ my faith with others to fulfill God's purposes.

- "The Lord is not slow in keeping his promise, as some understand slowness. Instead he is patient with you, not wanting anyone to perish, but everyone to come to _____" (2 Peter 3:9).

- **Key Verse**: "Pray also for me, that whenever I speak, words may be given me so that I will fearlessly make known the mystery of the gospel, for which I am an _____ in chains. Pray that I may declare it fearlessly, as I should" (Ephesians 6:19–20).

- (**Key Application #1**): Look for divine _____ _____.

- (**Key Application #2**): Start with a question and wait for the _____.

- **(Key Application #3)**: Share your _____ _____.

- **(Key Application #4)**: Acceptance of the good news is not your _____.

GETTING STARTED

Begin your discussion by reciting the key verse and key idea together as a group. On your first attempt, use your notes if you need help. On your second attempt, try to state them completely from memory.

KEY VERSE: "Pray also for me, that whenever I speak, words may be given me so that I will fearlessly make known the mystery of the gospel, for which I am an ambassador in chains. Pray that I may declare it fearlessly, as I should" (Ephesians 6:19–20).

KEY IDEA: I share my faith with others to fulfill God's purposes.

GROUP DISCUSSION

As a group, discuss your thoughts and feelings about the following declarations. Which statements are easy to declare with certainty? Which are more challenging? Why?

- I frequently share my faith with people who are not Christians.
- I try to live so that others will see Christ in my life.
- I know how to share my faith with non-Christians.
- I pray for non-Christians to accept Jesus Christ as their Lord and Savior.

Based on your group's dynamics and spiritual maturity, choose two or three questions that will lead to the best discussion about this week's key idea.

1. Is it possible to share your faith without saying a word? If so, how?

2. What present opportunities do you have to share your faith with people outside of the faith?

3. If what Jesus did through his death and resurrection is "good news," why do many believers hesitate to share it?

4. In what ways are you actively sharing your faith with unbelievers?

_____

_____

_____

_____

Read Genesis 12:1–4 and 2 Corinthians 5:14–21, and then choose one or two questions that will lead to the greatest discussion in your group.

1. In what ways do you see the world being blessed through God's people? In other words, how is the church positively affecting the world around it?

_____

_____

_____

2. Paul says we have been given a ministry of reconciliation. In your opinion, what does that mean?

_____

_____

_____

3. As ambassadors of Christ, we (the church) represent his character and desires to the world. In what ways are we representing him well? In what areas must we improve?

_____

_____

_____

CASE STUDY

Use the following case study as a model for a real-life situation where you might put this week's key idea into practice.

> Esperanza's story of redemption is powerful. God's grace radically changed the trajectory of her life from a destination of brokenness and addiction to a place of freedom and hope. Yet though she has found peace, her family and friends are headed for destruction. She feels a sense of responsibility to share her faith with them, but fear of doing or saying the wrong thing is holding her back.

Using the following key applications from this session, what could you say or do to help Esperanza?

KEY APPLICATION #1: Look for divine appointments.

KEY APPLICATION #2: Start with a question and wait for the invitation.

KEY APPLICATION #3: Share your story.

KEY APPLICATION #4: Acceptance of the good news is not your responsibility.

CLOSING PRAYER

Close your time together with prayer. Share your prayer requests with one another. Ask God to help you put this week's key idea into practice.

IN THE COMING DAYS

Be sure to read through the following personal study and complete the exercises.

VIDEO NOTES ANSWER KEY

faith / share / repentance / ambassador / appointments / invitation / story / responsibility

PERSONAL STUDY

Last week you examined the practice of giving away your resources. Perhaps you were challenged to loosen your hold on personal possessions, allowing them to be used for God's purposes. Before your next group meeting, complete the following study. Then take some time to evaluate your relationship with people outside of the Christian faith.

KEY QUESTION
HOW DO I SHARE MY FAITH WITH THOSE WHO DON'T KNOW GOD?

The Bible is clear there is a heaven and a hell and Jesus will return to judge all people and establish his eternal kingdom. The destination of people for all time is based on whether they receive forgiveness of their sins through Christ. He has provided the way of salvation, but people must embrace it individually for themselves. No one is "unsavable." But only those who receive salvation by faith in Christ in this life will be part of the eternal life to come.

This is why the call to share the gospel is so important! As Jesus' disciples, we are here on this earth to let people know—by how we live our lives and by the words we speak—what we know about Jesus. Year in and year out, decade after decade, statistics show that a majority of people become Christians because someone cared enough to share the gospel with them. Relationships have always been, and still are, God's primary path for bringing people into his kingdom. God has one plan for saving the world . . . and it is *us*.

For more than 2,000 years, Christianity has been one generation away from extinction. Yet the plan keeps working. Faith continues to move forward. Yes, it is true that people still die without having a relationship with Christ. But our mission remains clear: share the message with everyone we can. By responding to this call, we partner with God in his divine pursuit of broken souls.

"Jesus is

> 'the stone you builders rejected,
>> which has become the cornerstone.'

Salvation is found in no one else, for there is no other name under heaven given to mankind by which we must be saved" (Acts 4:11–12).

Pray also for me, that whenever I speak, words may be given me so that I will fearlessly make known the mystery of the gospel, for which I am an ambassador in chains. Pray that I may declare it fearlessly, as I should (Ephesians 6:19–20).

To the weak I became weak, to win the weak. I have become all things to all people so that by all possible means I might save some. I do all this for the sake of the gospel, that I may share in its blessings (1 Corinthians 9:22–23).

1. What should be your motivation in sharing your faith with others?

_____

_____

_____

2. How are your relationships part of God's plan to share the gospel with others?

_____

_____

_____

KEY IDEA

I SHARE MY FAITH WITH OTHERS TO FULFILL GOD'S PURPOSES

As believers in Christ, we each have different careers to make a living, but we all have the same job description: *ambassadors for Christ*. What do ambassadors do? They take God's message of reconciliation to the world. Across the street or across the globe, we speak God's message of salvation. How does this happen? By his power, he gives us the opportunity and the words. What is the appeal? God sent Jesus to die in our place. The debt we could never pay has been paid in full! This is why the gospel is called the *good news*.

When others see our faith, hope, and love—the way we *act like Jesus*—they are drawn to live in the same way. Over time, they begin to notice our relationship with God and want to have that relationship as well. We become a reflection of God's image to this world. As Jesus put it, we become "the salt of the earth" and "the light of the world" (Matthew 5:13–14).

We are to be the light of Christ and the good flavor of salt to the world. Doing so will require us to have the attitude of a humble servant. It will mean that we sometimes adapt our approach so we can meet the needs of those we are trying to reach. Many new believers in the early church were drawn to Christianity by the way those in the church served one another. In the same way, putting the needs of others before our own will serve as a beacon of light that will attract others to seek and find Christ.

> *"You are the salt of the earth. But if the salt loses its saltiness, how can it be made salty again? It is no longer good for anything, except to be thrown out and trampled underfoot.*
>
> *"You are the light of the world. A town built on a hill cannot be hidden. Neither do people light a lamp and put it under a bowl. Instead they put it on its stand, and it gives light to everyone in the house. In the same way, let your light shine before others, that they may see your good deeds and glorify your Father in heaven"* (Matthew 5:13–16).

> *Be wise in the way you act toward outsiders; make the most of every opportunity. Let your conversation be always full of grace, seasoned with salt, so that you may know how to answer everyone* (Colossians 4:5–6).

> *And he has committed to us the message of reconciliation. We are therefore Christ's ambassadors, as though God were making his appeal through us. We implore you on Christ's behalf: Be reconciled to God* (2 Corinthians 5:19–20).

Every day they continued to meet together in the temple courts. They broke bread in their homes and ate together with glad and sincere hearts, praising God and enjoying the favor of all the people. And the Lord added to their number daily those who were being saved (Acts 2:46–47).

1. What does it mean to be an *ambassador* for God?

   _____

   _____

   _____

   _____

2. Who in your life is an example of "salt and light" to those who need salvation?

   _____

   _____

   _____

   _____

KEY APPLICATION
WHAT DIFFERENCE THIS MAKES

You are never responsible to *save* but only to *share*. You role is to bring revelation, not to broker a response. You are to sow the seeds . . . and leave the harvest to God. But it is important to know how to share your faith. As a believer in Christ, you have a story to tell about how God saved you. It is your story—unique to you. The wonderful truth is that no one can debate or argue with us about its validity. Jesus made himself real to you. . . and you believe it.

There is a common denominator in all stories of coming to the faith. We were all lost and destined for hell. But Jesus found us and offered salvation. We received his gift and were saved. Case closed. So, no one's testimony is better than anyone else's. The result is always the same—we were saved from death and set on the path of God's kingdom.

Of course, when you present your story, it is also important to explain why the other person needs salvation. God's Word has the plan, so be prepared to share verses that will lead the other person to this realization. (The book of Romans is a great place to start—see 3:10, 23; 5:8; 6:23; 10:9–10, 13.) Basically, you need to explain that no one can get to God on his or her own because no one is righteous. But God has provided a way through the death of his Son on the cross. To accept this gift, we need to believe in our heart and confess with our mouth that Jesus is Lord. A simple prayer from the heart will do!

Regardless of how you choose to deliver the gospel, the most important element is that you are willing to share your faith. If you are willing and ready, God will bring the opportunities, because he longs to rescue people from sin and death. Nothing is more exhilarating than letting people in on the difference God makes and how true life is found in Jesus. When you are able to see someone point his or her life not only to God's kingdom but also to God's abundant life in the here and now, you fulfill the very reason that God has you on this earth.

> "I consider my life worth nothing to me; my only aim is to finish the race and complete the task the Lord Jesus has given me—the task of testifying to the good news of God's grace" (Acts 20:24).

If you declare with your mouth, "Jesus is Lord," and believe in your heart that God raised him from the dead, you will be saved. For it is with your heart that you believe and are justified, and it is with your mouth that you profess your faith and are saved (Romans 10:9–10).

How, then, can they call on the one they have not believed in? And how can they believe in the one of whom they have not heard? And how can they hear without someone preaching to them? And how can anyone preach unless they are sent? As it is written: "How beautiful are the feet of those who bring good news!" (Romans 10:14–15).

1. What motivates you to share your story of faith?

_____

_____

_____

_____

_____

_____

2. Why should you share your faith even if you think you might be rejected?

_____

_____

_____

_____

_____

_____

EVALUATE

As you conclude this personal study, use a scale of 1–6 to rate how strongly you believe the following statements (1 = no belief at all, 6 = complete confidence):

_____ I frequently share my faith with people who are not Christians.

_____ I try to live so that others will see Christ in my life.

_____ I know how to share my faith with non-Christians.

_____ I pray for non-Christians to accept Jesus Christ as their Lord and Savior.

TAKE ACTION

Memorizing Scripture is a valuable discipline for all believers to exercise. Spend a few minutes each day committing this week's key verse to memory.

KEY VERSE: "Pray also for me, that whenever I speak, words may be given me so that I will fearlessly make known the mystery of the gospel, for which I am an ambassador in chains. Pray that I may declare it fearlessly, as I should" (Ephesians 6:19–20).

Recite this week's key idea out loud. As you do, ask yourself, *Does my life reflect this statement?*

KEY IDEA: I share my faith with others to fulfill God's purposes.

Answer the following questions to help you apply this week's key idea to your own life.

1. How would this practice express itself in your life?

2. What visible attributes can be found in someone who regularly shares his or her faith?

3. What is impeding your ability to openly share your faith in Christ? How can you overcome this obstacle?

4. What step can you take this week to put yourself in a position to share what God has done in your life?

_____

_____

_____

_____

LEADER'S GUIDE

Thank you for your willingness to lead your group through this study! What you have chosen to do is valuable and will make a great difference in the lives of others. The rewards of being a leader are different from those participating, and we hope that as you lead you will find your own walk with Jesus deepened by this experience.

Act Like Jesus is an eight-session study built around video content and small-group interaction. As the group leader, just think of yourself as the host of a dinner party. Your job is to take care of your guests by managing all the behind-the-scenes details so that when everyone arrives, they can just enjoy time together.

As the group leader, your role is not to answer all the questions or reteach the content—the video and study guide will do most of that work. Your job is to guide the experience and cultivate your small group into a kind of teaching community. This will make it a place for members to process, question, and reflect—not receive more instruction.

Before your first meeting, make sure everyone in the group gets a copy of the study guide. This will keep everyone on the same page and help the process run more smoothly. If some group members are unable to purchase the guide, arrange it so that people can share the resource with other group members. Giving everyone access to all the material will position this study to be as rewarding an experience as possible. Everyone should feel free to write in his or her study guide and bring it to group every week.

SETTING UP THE GROUP

You will need to determine with your small group how long you want to meet each week so that you can plan your time accordingly. Generally, most groups like to meet for either ninety minutes or two hours, so you could use one of the following schedules:

SECTION	90 MINUTES	120 MINUTES
WELCOME (members arrive and get settled)	10 minutes	15 minutes
WATCH (watch the teaching material together and take notes)	15 minutes	15 minutes
DISCUSS (recite the key verse and key idea and discuss the study questions you selected)	40 minutes	60 minutes
CASE STUDY (go through the case study using the key applications for the session)	15 minutes	20 minutes
PRAY (close your time in prayer)	10 minutes	10 minutes

As the group leader, you will want to create an environment that encourages sharing and learning. A church sanctuary or formal classroom may not be as ideal as a living room in this regard, because those locations can feel formal and less intimate. No matter what setting you choose, provide enough comfortable seating for everyone, and, if possible, arrange the seats in a semicircle so everyone can see the video easily. This will make transition between the video and group conversation more efficient and natural.

Try to get to the meeting site early so you can greet participants as they arrive. Simple refreshments create a welcoming atmosphere and can be a wonderful addition to a group study evening. Try to take food and pet allergies into account to make your guests as comfortable as possible. You may also want to consider offering childcare to couples with children who want to attend. Finally, be sure your media technology is working properly. Managing these details up front will make the rest of your group experience flow smoothly and provide a welcoming space to engage the content of *Act Like Jesus*.

STRUCTURING THE GROUP TIME

Once everyone has arrived, it's time to begin the group. Here are some simple tips to make your group time healthy, enjoyable, and effective.

First, begin the meeting with a short prayer and remind the group members to put their phones on silent. This is a way to make sure you can all be present with one another and with God. Next, watch the video and instruct the participants to follow along in their guides and take notes. After the video teaching, have the group recite the key verse and key idea together before moving on to the discussion questions.

Encourage all the group members to participate in the discussion, but make sure they know they don't have to do so. As the discussion progresses, you may want to follow up with comments such as, "Tell me more about that," or, "Why did you answer that way?" This will allow the group participants to deepen their reflections and invite meaningful sharing in a nonthreatening way.

Note that you have been given multiple questions to use in each session, and you do not have to use them all or even follow them in order. Feel free to pick and choose questions based on either the needs of your group or how the conversation is flowing. Also, don't be afraid of silence. Offering a question and allowing up to thirty seconds of silence is okay. It allows people space to think about how they want to respond and also gives them time to do so.

As group leader, you are the boundary keeper for your group. Do not let anyone (yourself included) dominate the group time. Keep an eye out for group members who might be tempted to "attack" folks they disagree with or try to "fix" those having struggles. These kinds of behaviors can derail a group's momentum, so they need to be steered in a different direction. Model active listening and encourage everyone in your group to do the same. This will make your group time a safe space and create a positive community.

CONCLUDING THE GROUP TIME

Each session in *Act Like Jesus* ends with a case study to help the group members process the key concepts and apply them to a real-life situation. At the conclusion of session one, invite the group members to complete the between-sessions personal studies for that week. Explain that you will be providing some time before the video teaching next week for anyone to share insights. (Do this as part of the opening "Welcome" beginning in session two, right before you watch the video.) Let them know sharing is optional.

Thank you again for taking the time to lead your group and helping them to understand what it means to *Act Like Jesus*. You are making a difference in the lives of others and having an impact for the kingdom of God!

If You Want to Grow in Your Faith, You Must Engage God's Word

What you believe in your heart will define who you become. God wants you to become like Jesus—it is the most truthful and powerful way to live—and the journey to becoming like Jesus begins by thinking like Jesus.

Jesus compared the Christian life to a vine. He is the vine; you are the branches. If you remain in the vine of Christ, over time you will produce amazing and scrumptious fruit for all to see and taste. You begin to act like Jesus, and become more like Jesus.

In the **Believe Bible Study Series**, bestselling author and pastor Randy Frazee helps you ask three big questions:

- What do I believe and why does it matter?
- How can I put my faith into action?
- Am I becoming the person God wants me to be?

Each of the three eight-session studies in this series include video teaching from Randy Frazee and a study guide with video study notes, group discussion questions, Scripture reading, and activities for personal growth and reflection.

As you journey through this study series, whether in a group or on your own, one simple truth will become undeniably clear: what you believe drives everything.

Available now at your favorite bookstore, or streaming video on StudyGateway.com.

What Do I Believe and Why Does It Matter?

What you believe drives everything. The way you behave, the habits you form, the character that defines you at your core—all are driven by what you believe.

It's not enough to believe something as the right answer; you must believe it as a way of life.

The *Think Like Jesus* eight-session video Bible study helps you understand the key beliefs of Christianity that, when embraced in the mind and heart, create true change in your individual life, in the church, and in the world.

Grounded in carefully selected Scripture, *Think Like Jesus* will take you on a journey to become more like Jesus in your beliefs. This revised study, adapted from Part 1 of the *Believe* churchwide study, includes an updated study guide, with new content and questions adapted from the existing *Believe Study Guide* and *Think, Act, Be Like Jesus* by Randy Frazee.

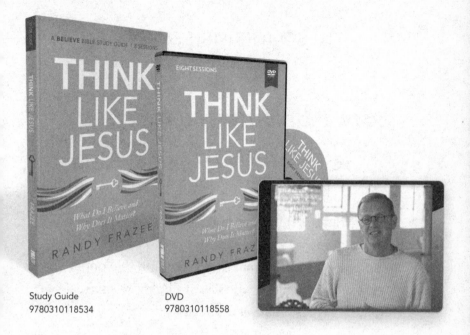

Study Guide
9780310118534

DVD
9780310118558

Sessions Include:

1. Who Is God?
2. Does God Care About Me?
3. How Do I Have a Relationship with God?
4. How Does the Bible Guide My Life?
5. Who Am I in Christ?
6. What is the Purpose of the Church?
7. How Does God Value People?
8. What Is Eternity Going to Be Like?

Available now at your favorite bookstore,
or streaming video on StudyGateway.com.

Am I Becoming the Person God Wants Me to Be?

Jesus wants you to bear fruit that glorifies God and brings great joy to you and to others. For this to happen, you must remain in Christ. And the longer you remain in community with Christ, the more spiritual fruit, or virtues, you will produce.

The *Be Like Jesus* eight-session video Bible study illuminates the virtues—the outward life changes in you—that are formed by the beliefs (*Think Like Jesus*) and cemented through the practices (*Act Like Jesus*). It is a grand cycle that shapes you into the image of Christ more and more every day.

Grounded in carefully selected Scripture, *Be Like Jesus* will take you on a journey to become more like Jesus in your behaviors. This revised study, adapted from Part 3 of the *Believe* churchwide study, includes an updated video study and new content and questions adapted from the existing *Believe Study Guide* and *Think, Act, Be Like Jesus* by Randy Frazee.

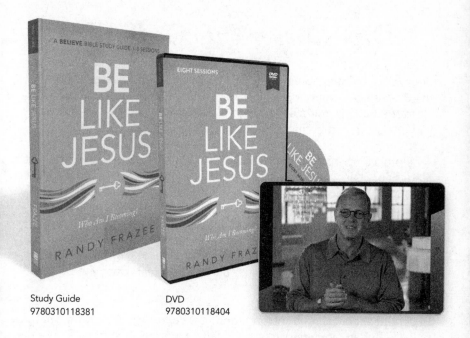

Study Guide
9780310118381

DVD
9780310118404

Sessions Include:

1. How Does God Want Me to Love Others?
2. What Will Give Me True Joy?
3. How Do I Find Real Peace?
4. How Does God Free Me from Sinful Habits?
5. How Can I Maintain Hope During Hardships?
6. How Can I Be Patient with Others?
7. Why Should I Be Loyal to Others?
8. How Can I Be Considerate of Others?

Available now at your favorite bookstore,
or streaming video on StudyGateway.com.